Hooray for Grandparents!

Hooray for Grandparents!

Ideas for Keeping Close, Building Traditions, and Creating Lasting Memories

JAY PAYLEITNER

CHRONICLE BOOKS
SAN FRANCISCO

Scriptures are taken from the HOLY BIBLE, NEW LIVING TRANSLATION. Copyright © 1996, 2004, 2007 by Tyndale House Foundation. Used by permission of Tyndale House Publishers, Inc., Carol Stream, Illinois, 60188. All rights reserved.

Library of Congress Cataloging-in-Publication Data
Names: Payleitner, Jay K., author.
Title: Hooray for grandparents : ideas for keeping close, building traditions, and creating lasting memories/Jay Payleitner.
Description: San Francisco : Chronicle Books, 2022.
Identifiers: LCCN 2021053284 (print) | LCCN 2021053285 (ebook) | ISBN 9781797212975 (hardback) | ISBN 9781797215402 (ebook)
Subjects: LCSH: Grandparents. | Grandparent and child. | Families.
Classification: LCC HQ759.9 .P39 2022 (print) | LCC HQ759.9 (ebook) | DDC 306.874/5--dc23/eng/20211228
LC record available at https://lccn.loc.gov/2021053284
LC ebook record available at https://lccn.loc.gov/2021053285

Manufactured in China.

MIX
Paper from responsible sources
FSC™ C008047

Design by Katherine Yao and Angie Kang.

10 9 8 7 6 5 4 3 2 1

Chronicle books and gifts are available at special quantity discounts to corporations, professional associations, literacy programs, and other organizations. For details and discount information, please contact our premiums department at corporatesales@chroniclebooks.com or at 1-800-759-0190.

Chronicle Books LLC
680 Second Street
San Francisco, California 94107
www.chroniclebooks.com

Dedicated, of course,
to our grandkids:

*Judah, Jackson, Emerson, Gideon,
Reese, Nolan, Finn, and Nixon*

TABLE OF CONTENTS

INTRODUCTION

AS A COMMITTED PARENT, YOU RAISED A KID. Or two. Or ten. You've witnessed all kinds of things while making a life and watching your family grow. You're smart and experienced and you know how to roll with the punches and get things done. Not much surprises you anymore.

But there's nothing like being a grandparent.

Just thinking about that next generation of your family, memories from the past and dreams for the future come into clear focus. You find yourself right in the middle of overflowing wonderment, chaos, and adventure.

You realize that much of who you are and what you've accomplished has been preparing you for this grand feat. In many ways, being a grandparent is a culmination of your life story. This opportunity to leave a legacy becomes part of who you are. It changes you.

Maybe you've never noticed, but a kind of rebirth happens when grandkids arrive on the scene. Hard-charging CEOs, gruff steelworkers, disciplined operating-room nurses, veteran educators, and gritty journalists all turn to mush when they hold their new grandson or walk down a garden path with their young granddaughter. Even a two-minute video chat with a kindergartner can leave a seasoned senior a little awestruck.

Why is that? Why are your heart and mind suddenly overflowing with unprecedented emotions?

Maybe because you see the big picture. You are aware of the joys, trials, laughter, and tears that lie ahead for those kids and their parents.

Maybe because you have a stockpile of memories that were almost forgotten but have suddenly flooded back as you recall your own history of parenting flubs, frustrations, wonders, and discoveries.

Maybe it's pride in your own son or daughter, seeing the family they're building, and delighting in the chance to cheer them on from a front-row seat.

But the most likely reason is that you're experiencing an entirely new kind of love for the first time.

It's spilling over in a totally unexpected way. You're overwhelmed. Grandparental love—if that's a word—is a mystical force that simply cannot be explained. You've been sacrificing, scheming, and striving on behalf of your family for decades, and you didn't think you had any more to give. But you do! And your desire to give and give even more is unimaginable.

By the way, if it hasn't hit you yet, that's okay. That overflow of love may not strike full force until some future milestone. Like the first time that baby runs to you or says your name. Or when they share a child-size secret with only you. Or when they come into a room and you encounter a flashback of your own son or daughter.

This book is going to help you endure and embrace all those emotions, especially during those moments when being a grandparent has the potential to be the most challenging or the most rewarding.

As you establish your legacy, never forget the love and nurturing you bestow on your grandchildren will have an impact on their lives and their world for generations to come.

Enjoy it all. The gift you've been given. The season of life. The insights and emotions stirred up by this little book. And your well-deserved title: **GRANDPARENT!**

1
REINFORCE FAMILY TRADITIONS

As a grandparent, you may find yourself in a ringside seat watching as your own children—the parents of your grandkids—frantically, lovingly, and sometimes methodically devote themselves to surviving the here and now.

Their single-minded focus is no surprise. Parenting—as you well know—can be a nonstop battle of just trying to get through today and then crashing into bed with just enough energy to ask yourself, *What's the schedule tomorrow?*

For young parents, that is where their focus should be. But that begs the question, *What should* you *be focusing on?*

Certainly, you might prudently come alongside those new or struggling parents with encouragement, small gestures, well-timed visits, labors of love, gentle insights, and an occasional financial investment.

But the primary answer to that question helps define what could possibly be your greatest role as a grandparent. While Mom and Dad think short-term, Grandma and Grandpa have the luxury of thinking long-term. That's a key part of building your legacy.

One of the most satisfying legacy-building techniques is remembering, keeping, and documenting family traditions. Perhaps more than anything else, your family traditions are what keep generations connected and lines of communication open. When a tradition comes up on the calendar, every member of the family knows to stop and take heed.

Some traditions happen naturally. Many are rediscovered when a family welcomes a new baby. For example, a multigenerational baby shower. A decades-old baby blanket being passed down. A colorful mobile that hung over Dad's crib now hangs from the ceiling in the baby's room. A christening or baptism.

If no traditions come to mind related to welcoming new babies into the family, then consider this an opportunity to lay some new groundwork in that area. Take a moment to brainstorm ideas and don't forget to consider your cultural heritage. Many traditions revolve around food, artwork, jewelry, music, prayer, books, nature, crafting, and woodworking. It might be as simple as preparing a welcome-home meal of favorite comfort food for the new parents. Imagine creating and dedicating a quilt, woodcarving, original song, needlepoint, or some other gift for the new little

WARM FUZZY TRADITIONS

The very word *tradition* evokes images of ceremonial activities at annual events, especially around holidays. Go ahead and start there, but don't end there. Consider establishing smaller family traditions that are much more frequent than just once a year. For example, at the end of every video chat, make the same loving gesture: a thumbs-up, an ear tug, or a blown kiss. At the end of every in-person visit, do a silly handshake or high five, give noogies or bear hugs, or give your grandchild a small collectible memento. At every shared meal, make a toast, ask a blessing, or initiate an engaging roundtable activity. Once a week, text a joke or word of encouragement to your entire family. These kinds of smaller traditions speak to the heart and leave family members looking forward to the next time you connect.

one. That's a tradition that could be repeated for each grandchild that comes along.

As your grandkids grow, expect dozens of traditions to come to mind. You may not call them such, but that's what they are, and those traditions become enormously important to kids. Examples include going to the same lake every summer. Family talent shows. Touch football on Thanksgiving. Taco Tuesdays. Pizza Fridays. A secret family handshake. Gifting silver dollars on special occasions. Stopping for ice cream during bike rides. Sitting in the same pew at church. Visiting the zoo every summer. Toasting with hot chocolate every New Year's Eve. Stopping by Nana's gravestone on her birthday. Making s'mores in the fireplace. Posing for photos on the first day of school.

Traditions help make a family. And it makes sense for grandparents to crown themselves as "Official Keepers of Traditions." If you accept that role, you'll establish yourself as trustworthy and consistent. Your family will honor you and follow your instruction because they have come to rely on you day after day, year after year, generation after generation. ●

Most of the time, when a grandparent revives an overlooked family custom or tradition, that idea is welcomed with unanimous approval. If not, you'll know soon enough.

2

EYE TO EYE
AND HEART
TO HEART

Where might you do your best grandparenting? Have you identified a special place you can talk and dream with any or all of your grandchildren? Specifically, someplace in or around your home, like a workshop, garden, home office, porch swing, or kitchen sink.

Your goal is to make the most of that precious time you have with those kids you love so much. One of the secrets to identifying your special place is to find a spot where you can engage literally on the same level. Eye to eye. Shoulder to shoulder. Heart to heart.

When they're newborns, that might be a rocking chair where you can snuggle them up in your arms, breathing in their scent and resting them on your chest. (That includes you, Grandpa!) Fresh out of the womb, babies focus best on images 8 to 15 inches (20 to 38 cm) away. That's the distance to your face when you're in proper snuggling position.

When they're toddlers, getting on the same level means lying on the carpet as they race Hot Wheels, connect Lego, animate stuffed animals, or scribble masterpieces. That's part of entering their often magical world.

When they turn three, you'll want to invest in two different stools. One that sits them up at your kitchen table so they can join life with the rest of the family. That's also the stool they may drag over to sit by you at your desk or sewing machine. The second stool is 10 inches (25 cm) high. They will quickly learn to pull that step stool up to your kitchen counter or workbench. How else are they going to learn to crack an egg, roll out pizza dough, or pound a nail? Mom and Dad may not have time for such nonsense. But teaching your grandchild a critical life skill might be the most important thing you do this month.

Seeing eye to eye becomes even more critical (and rewarding) when they are actually the same height as you. Those intentional connections during their newborn, toddler, and school-age years are

Hooray for

hugely important for setting the tone for future conversations. More times than you might think, grandparents will be a guiding light for a middle schooler or high schooler navigating tough life transitions.

Time spent with a teenage grandchild may still be in the kitchen, garden, or workshop, and it may still involve some kind of cooking, planting, or construction project, but those young people know it's about more than that. That's why they love to hang out with you. At Grandma's or Grandpa's house, they are counting on *life lessons* and *lessons about life* overlapping. Over the years, you have demonstrated that life goes on when you burn a pie crust or hit your thumb with a hammer. That's good to know when a young person gets dumped by a girlfriend or cut from a basketball team.

You have earned the right to look them in the eye and say something heartfelt like, "Well, *that's* not good. But you know what? Our family has a history of handling disappointments pretty well and we usually find something even better right around the next corner."

Coming from Mom or Dad, that kind of advice can sound lame. But from grandparents—seeing eye to eye and speaking heart to heart—those words sound like wisdom for the ages and can make a world of difference. •

Grandparents can deliver a myriad of truths that parents are afraid to speak.

3

STOP AND SMELL THE BABY SHAMPOO

I'm a work-at-home writer and have been since our kids were little. How I was able concentrate enough to write ads, radio scripts, marketing material—and later books—seems impossible to imagine. We never had a big house, so the typical ruckus created by five active rug rats was always within earshot.

Client deadlines and looming mortgage payments may have helped me focus, but I have to give my wife, Rita, much credit.

Somehow she corralled the kids and kept them from the door of my home office. Looking back, it was a lifetime ago. More accurately, eight lifetimes ago.

With the birth of each of our eight grandchildren, Rita has eagerly made herself available to cuddle and entertain any or all of those little ones at any time. As with our own kids, this tends to occur just outside my office door.

Every season and school year has led to a different arrangement, but mostly it has been Rita getting her fix of holding babies. (That's one of her favorite things to do, which is why we opened our home to ten foster babies over the years.)

For me and my own productivity, the difference between those two seasons of my life is astounding. Back in the day, I somehow would still get a ton of work done with my own kids in the next room. Today, not so much. Even as I type these words, my nine-month-old grandson, Finn, is on the other side of the door, just a few steps away, and it's taking every ounce of willpower not to get up from my desk chair and hang out with him. I know, very soon, I will succumb to temptation. When I open that office door, my young grandson will gasp with delight and his little round face will turn in my direction knowing what's next. Chief—that's what my grandkids call me—will come close, swoop him into the air, burble his cheek, howl, sing, and grunt, causing Finn to squeal with delight. And most importantly, for this old soul, I will breathe in the tangible scent and vitality of youth.

Not to say, twenty-some years ago, I never took a break in my day to spend time with my own kids. Especially after finishing a chapter, getting off a long phone call, or sending a carefully worded email, I would release my office shackles and take a moment to listen to a tale from their school day or shoot some driveway hoops. But that was as a dad. I knew that entering my kids' world was good for them.

As a grandfather, it's all about my own selfish desires. Every interaction is a cherished blessing. Parents tend not to savor the moments. They probably should, but there's so much to be done and the "moments" aren't quite so obvious. Moms and dads may overlook the joyful blurs of bliss hidden in the endless routine of dirty dishes, unwashed clothes, wiping noses, homework hassles, carpool schedules, and collapsing in exhaustion when the kids are finally asleep.

But for Grandma and Grandpa, your life experience tells a different story. You know that the fondest memories are made in the busyness of life. But that requires you to stop and smell the baby shampoo. Or the fresh-picked dandelion. Or the unique scent of a middle schooler's sweatshirt. If you don't pause, the magical moments are missed.

So before I go and swoop up Finn into a fit of giggles, allow me to offer this exhortation. When your grandchildren are near, use every sense to take them in. Hold them. Listen to them. Look into their eyes. Kiss them. Breathe in their aura—especially babies who smell like talcum, lotion, and shampoo.

Surrender to it. Pursue it. You may not live close enough or have the schedule flexibility to babysit two or three days per week, but don't let that be an excuse. If your spouse—or your inner voice—announces, "Let's go see the grandkids," don't hesitate. Drop what you're doing, get in the car, jump on the plane, and go get your grandkid fix.

Your grandchildren and their parents need it. Almost as much as you do. ●

4
PICK YOUR NEW NAME

This is no small decision. Whatever your grandchild calls you may very well be the way you are addressed by dozens of people for the rest of your life. That includes your grandkids, sons, daughters, sons-in-law, daughters-in-law, other members of the family, and perhaps many of the strangers you meet from this day forward.

The options for names are endless, and you certainly have the right to make your own choice. Be warned. If you're not proactive in the area, you may end up with a nickname that doesn't quite feel right. Not to worry, though. As soon as your granddaughter or grandson starts calling that name, your heart will melt and you'll be gladdened every time you hear it.

If you are approaching that time when your grandparenting name is about to be set in stone, what's your next step? Some grandparent-naming stories will help clarify the process.

For fifty-four years my mom and dad were Marge and Ken. For the following thirty years or so, they were Mimi and Papa. That's how they introduced themselves. That's how they signed cards. That's what they called each other. How did they get those names? My older sister Mary Kay chose them without consulting anyone. When my parents' first grandchild, my niece Katie, was just learning to talk, Mary Kay taught her to say "Mimi" and "Papa." The names stuck and thankfully they worked quite nicely.

My wife, Rita, was looking forward to being a grandmother for more than a few years. When our first grandchild Jackson finally came along, she didn't attempt to disguise her identity with something like "Birdy, "Marnie," or "Ri-Ri." She went all in with the request to be called "Grama." Perfect.

With similar intent, I had made a preemptive decision to go with "Gramps." I liked that single strong syllable. That name lasted about six months. Two of my daughters-in-law got together and dubbed me "Chief." I'm not a cop, firefighter, or Native American, but it totally works for me. Call me Chief, and I'll gladly respond.

When it comes to choosing your new name, the critical window is the first few months after your first grandchild is born. For a while, lullabies and hugs are the priority. But you will want to decide on your new name before the baby's language skills start to develop. Way before they talk, they'll learn sounds and words, and you

"SO WHAT DO THEY CALL YOU?"

Of course, this author has no idea what grandparenting title you're going to choose (or was chosen long ago). Chatting with other grandparents over the years, a marvelous profusion of creative names have come to my attention—anything from Oma and Grandpapa to Kiki and G-daddy. If you have been blessed (or saddled) with a creative nickname, I hope you'll track me down at jaypayleitner.com and let me know. I'll add it to my collection.

Occasionally, you will find yourself in conversation with another grandparent, exchanging anecdotes or digital photos. Feel free to steal one of my favorite questions to ask: "So what do they call you?" Inevitably, their face lights up as they share their well-earned title. Whether it's fairly traditional or completely off the wall, there's always a sense of mirth and wistfulness in the answer.

If their first grandchild is a newborn or not yet speaking, it's possible their grandparenting name has not been established. As a fellow grandparent, you have the responsibility to share some of the insight in this chapter. Let them know their new name will follow them for years to come and may very well be etched on their gravestone.

want them to know the name of the nice person hugging them up and singing those lullabies. So don't wait too long.

Think about it. Talk it over. Do a search online for names that are both trendy and traditional. Consider names that reflect your national and family heritage.

Another reason to think about this sooner rather than later is because—after much debate—you may finally decide on a wonderful title only to discover that the other grandparents have already claimed that name. That would be close to tragic.

So enjoy the process, pick a good one, and look forward to the time when your grandkids burst through your front door and say something like, "Chief! Chief! Guess what!" ●

There's no sweeter sound than a grandchild running through your front door calling your name.

5
MARKING
MILESTONES

Especially with newborns and toddlers, most new parents are slightly obsessed with growth metrics. They know the weight and length of their baby at birth and will dutifully monitor those numbers for weeks. After that early crisis of concern, they anxiously look for other clues that their baby is maturing fast enough. Parents especially can't help but think, *When do they smile, roll over, crawl, clap their hands, take their first cute little baby steps, and know their ABCs?* Potty training—getting that tyke out of diapers ASAP—is an especially high-priority milestone for parents.

Well, Grandma and Grandpa, unless that youngster's parents ask for your opinion, you need to let them determine the schedule and methodology of reaching such milestones. When it comes to toilet training, the opinions of so-called national experts are constantly changing, which means inserting yourself in the debate is almost always asking for trouble. Moreover, if you're babysitting the little one, you're going to want to faithfully match the routine used by the baby's parents and use the same names for body parts and the activity itself. Which means you may find yourself offering bribes, enduring new and unusual rituals, speaking unfamiliar terms, or changing way too many diapers than you think are necessary. I'm fairly sure you can handle it.

Beyond reliving the horrors of potty training, it's probably healthy for you to reflect back on some of your own emotions regarding the maturing progress of your own children so many years ago. Recalling that season of your life will give you the valuable character trait of empathy. Which, by the way, is a healthy skill this world could use a little more of. In this case, empathy helps you (1) feel what your kids are going through, (2) recall some of your own experiences as a young parent, and (3) remind yourself to be available, but not meddlesome.

Chances are you will remember those days as an odd mix of research, worry, pride, and comparing notes with other parents. Decades later, your perspective has evolved. You now know every child is different, and that while parents should generally be aware of how their little one is progressing, panicking is never the answer. A little patience goes a long way.

If you perceive your grandchild's parents are stressing over early milestones, you can offer great comfort with just a few words. Careful now, don't go with your first instinct, which is often to minimize their concerns. Even though you know it's true, please don't say, "Just be patient, he'll catch up," or "Don't worry. Every baby has their own schedule."

When you dismiss the parents' concerns, you're not being helpful and you're actually pushing them away at a time they need you most. The good news is that—because you don't see the baby every day—you've been given a wonderfully valuable perspective. Without exaggerating or outright lying, you can—sincerely—provide confirmation that those parents just need to *stay the course*. If it's been two weeks since your last interaction, you can enthusiastically confirm that your grandson or granddaughter is "doing so much more" than the last time you saw them. Then back up your welcome statement with specific examples of advancing maturity, including the baby's longer attention spans, brighter smiles, increased eye contact, clearer verbalization, and whatever else you notice.

Grandma and Grandpa, your instinct is understandable. You want to speak truth into the lives of your children regarding the lack of progress when it comes to your grandchildren's milestones. You think you're being helpful when you point out your grandchild's stutter, lazy eye, or hyperactivity. But what you don't realize is that the parents are probably well aware of the condition and, by the way, the terms you will probably use are currently considered outdated and even hurtful. Even using terms recommended by clinicians—*childhood-onset fluency disorder, amblyopia*, and *ADHD* or *hypersensitivity*—will not likely sit well with Mom and Dad.

Which brings us back full circle to this idea. As devoted grandparents, your job is to love unconditionally and be available with wisdom and experience *when called upon*.

Feel free to do your research. Even do your own tracking of your grandchildren's progress at reaching milestones. But keep it to yourself. Be patient. The more you engage with your grandchildren, the more likely Mom and Dad will be to ask your opinion. That's when you can share your best advice. Even then, go easy. Listen more than speak. Ask questions. Don't diagnose or recommend a specific course of action. Be a gentle and encouraging sounding board for the parents regarding recommended treatments, therapies, and medications.

It's worth the reminder. Medical technologies and psychosocial understandings have advanced since the days when you were raising little ones. But also sometimes kids will be kids, and often they do "grow out of it."

In conclusion, when it comes to milestones, the recommended four-point plan for grandparents is empathy, availability, patience, and unconditional love. •

6

THE RECENT EVOLUTION OF GRAND-PARENTING

My father's mother was mostly amusing. Nana was not the proverbial huggy, storytelling, and pie-making grandmother. But she tried. I remember proudly showing her one of my school report cards and she said, "Well, as long as you passed." Even as a fifth grader, I thought, *What the heck! It's all As and Bs. What do you want?* Still, she was generally approachable and good-natured.

Grandpa Fritz, on the other hand, was a bit intimidating. Barrel-chested and mostly serious, his slight German accent only added to his larger-than-life presence. He was the night shift supervisor at the American Motors plant in Kenosha, Wisconsin. Family lore suggests he was regularly offered promotions that would have brought him back to the day shift, but he turned them down. Working when the big bosses were around would have taken away some of his autonomy. He liked being in charge.

Because we never talked, I don't know anything about his youth or his own parents or grandparents. I wished I would have asked him about his experience in World War I, but is that sparsity of communication on me? I don't think so. Neither can I blame Grandpa Fritz.

Comparing notes with other men of my generation, the impression that our grandparents—especially grandfathers—were stoic, detached, and not fully engaged was not unusual. For the most part, I think today's culture has done a 180-degree turn when it comes to those generational connections.

As a twenty-first-century grandparent, there's high probability you are quite capable of holding your new grandbaby, and not just for a photo op. You may even tickle toes and burble their tummy.

With preschoolers, you're going to get down on their level on the grass or carpet. To keep up with your growing grandkids, you'll wade into creeks, chase down Frisbees, and ride go-karts and snowmobiles. Heck, you might even climb rock walls, go zip-lining, and organize water balloon fights.

That's all good stuff. Do those things. I one hundred percent approve of grandparents who goof around with their grandchildren. But if you think you know where this chapter is going, think again.

We're going to flip this script. I submit that today's young people—your grandchildren—could use a few more role models with the commanding presence exhibited by my grandfather. Yes, you should bring fun and games into the grandparenting equation. But you're much more than that. Never surrender your foundational role as patriarch or matriarch of the family. That role—that only you can play—establishes an identity for your grandchildren that will serve them when they begin to question their purpose or start to get sidetracked by outside forces.

You are the conduit of your family's heritage. You're passing on a pedigree of ambition, honor, and integrity. In other words, the (*insert your last name here*) family stands for something. And it's worth passing on.

If it's in you, convey that idea with spoken or written words. Use words like *heritage, legacy,* and *family history.* But even more critical is your capacity as a role model living out all the best characteristics of your lineage. Can you see how there is value in that attitude? From both Grandpa and Grandma?

Then here's the big idea of this chapter. Let's already assume you will be more playful, engaging, and hands-on than your grandparents. So you get no points for that. But you still need to bring to your family some of the same purposeful gravitas demonstrated by your grandfather or grandmother. Sure, maybe they could have loosened up a little, but there's no doubt they loved you, and when they looked at you, they saw the future. They were doing their best to make sure the heritage they received from their parents and grandparents was passed on with conviction and resolve. ●

Young people who know their heritage will honor their family.

7
DISPLAY YOUR PHOTO ALBUMS PROUDLY

As your grandkids approach the teenage years, they will secretly marvel at your photo albums. By that time—because of the current prevalence of smartphones—they will have already taken more photographs than you will ever take. But very few of their pics exist beyond the digital realm.

What's more, there's an underlying fear that "the cloud" that supposedly safely preserves all those precious memories will someday come crashing down and the gazillion photos taken by millennials are going to be lost forever.

Good news. All your albums of photos taken with your Kodaks and Nikons are safe and sound. Or at least they should be. If those clunky binders are in the basement or garage gathering dust or facing an onslaught of mold or mildew, I urge you to rescue them today.

In most cases, the photos within are one-of-a kind and irreplace-able. Sure, many are out of focus and off-center. Your albums likely contain page after page of cheesy posed images snapped at graduations, during holidays, and on front porch steps. You might wonder why you still have that photo of a great-uncle whose name you can't remember standing at a barbecue grill, holding up a stringer of blue gills, or wearing a Hawaiian shirt, white socks, and sandals. You'll most certainly come across undated vacation snapshots featuring unrecognizable family members standing in front of statues, memorials, and tourist traps. But unlike your grandchildren's phones, those albums at least won't contain a single duck-face selfie.

What's the real benefit of those ancient photo albums? Like so many artifacts in and around your home, it's all about sharing and creating memories with your grandkids. Connecting the future to the past. Your own children have seen the photos and only pause

"BACK IN MY DAY..."

You'll want to go easy on using the expression, but picture-taking is an excellent example of when you might explain how things were different "back in my day." Your grandchild's phone cost hundreds of dollars, but the pictures they take are essentially free. Conversely, the photos found in your old albums cost you about fifty cents each for film and processing. Which means you didn't take nine shots of every photo opportunity and you really didn't know whether someone blinked until you got the photos back from the drugstore. That's also why you saved every single print from every roll of film. Even if heads are cut off, every smile is forced, and Grandpa is clearly yelling, "Take the damn picture!"

to take a closer look at the ones that display their own younger faces. But once in a while a grandchild will be in the mood to investigate the visual heritage from which they evolved. You can't force it on them, but just having those albums available will pique their curiosity.

So make sure those albums are accessible. Next time a grandkid is coming over, intentionally pull out the quirkiest album you have and set it on the corner of the kitchen table. Let them discover it.

Very likely, they'll pause several times as they turn pages. They'll study a decades-old photo of their mom or dad and be the first one to notice a sapling in one photo that has become a towering oak in your side yard. Don't be surprised if, while looking at a photo of you, they see themselves. That's a moment you'll both remember.

Each time they pause, see if you can share a story behind the event captured in that fading print. If a conversation goes on for several minutes, go ahead and pull back the acetate sheet, or slip that photograph from its mounting corners, and tell your grandchild to take it home. Sure, it will leave a blank spot on that album page, but the cherished image will now be out in the world doing what photos are meant to do.

There's a good chance your curious and thoughtful grandchild will repurpose that photograph with a digital scan to be shared on some app you may never see. Which means it might be out there in the virtual universe forever.

As for the rest of the albums? Wherever you happen to live in the years to come, drag them along. The entire collection. Feel free to organize, consolidate, or gently write names and dates on the back of photos, if you must. But leaving them "as is" works too.

In the distant future, the next generation may end up tossing most of those albums in some dumpster. They'll feel a bit guilty about it. And nostalgic. Which means they'll interrupt their immense undertaking and spend an afternoon paging through those albums and reflecting on the past, the present, and the future. ●

Faded photographs come to life when shared with a grandchild.

8
SHARING
YOUR
GRANDKIDS

Hate to break it to you, but you are not the only grandparent in your grandchild's life. Which means your obligatory goal—being the favorite grandparent—is not going to be awarded to you just for showing up. You've got work to do.

Who else is in the race? Every family is different, but near the top of that list is probably your own spouse. Then, of course, your child's partner has parents. In addition, there may be other former partners, in-laws, or favorite aunts or uncles who may be climbing in the rankings of favorite.

Competition may even come from some neighbor or babysitter you don't even know. One day, you might be playing Candy Land with little Sophia and she'll say something like, "GamGam lets me go over the rainbow bridge every time." When that happens, you need to track down that grandmothering impostor and insist that GamGam play by the rules of Candy Land and stop trying to edge you out as fave grandparent.

In truth, positive role models and playmates of any age are good for your grandkids. I can attest to feelings of both gratitude and jealousy when it comes to the other grandparents in the lives of Judah, Jackson, Emerson, Gideon, Reese, Nolan, Finn, and Nixon. I also know Rita and I are blessed beyond measure by those other grandparents, and there's plenty of love to go around.

For context, three of our grandkids live in our hometown. Two live in the next county, but Rita and I are still the closest grandparents. Three live 150 miles (240 km) away in the same city as the "other" grandparents.

Proximity is not the only factor in connecting with grandkids. As stated earlier, Rita excels at snuggling with newborns. Anytime she is holding one of her infant grandkids, she's the favorite.

I know I'm in the running for favorite grandparent when kids are between the ages of three and five. That's because my natural instinct is to give horsey rides, listen to their stories, wrestle, oooh and aaah over caterpillars, give noogies, and make sandcastles and balloon animals. When they mature beyond that young age, sometimes I make the mistake of trying way too hard to teach them lessons and life principles, which doesn't always go over so well, causing me to lose points.

You might be in competition with grandparents who have an advantage of living with the grandkids or having more time and money. They may have fun stuff, like a trampoline, swimming pool, basketball hoop, giant backyard, or jungle gym. Maybe they live on a farm, own a boat, or have a beach house. Grandparents who live in a skyscraper in the exciting big city definitely have an advantage with some kids, especially older grandchildren.

To claim the coveted title, you might find yourself allowing unlimited ice cream, video marathons, or bedtimes that go against Mom and Dad's instructions. I don't recommend it. On the other hand, it's probably okay if your rules are a little more lenient than at home. Furthermore, cash bribery is not allowed.

Let me reiterate: Be grateful for every person of any age who truly loves your grandchildren . . . and for every person they truly love. I really do appreciate the wonderful grandparents all my grandchildren have on "the other side."

Still, I do not take the quest to be "the favorite" lightly. If this book is picked up and read by Richard, Linda, Dave, Deb, Marty, Cathy, or even Rita, let me assure you the battle is on. ●

Even in your quest to be the favorite grandparent, do your best not to pick a favorite grandchild.

9
DON'T BUY JUNK

One of the great joys of grandparenting is strolling through a dollar store with a five-year-old. You can say "Yes" three or four times to their wide-eyed requests and it'll cost you less than five bucks. Later that afternoon, when the dress-up plastic jewelry falls to pieces or the water pistol dribbles instead of squirts, there should be no panic, no tears, and no marching back to the store for a refund.

Helping your grandchildren learn that life goes on when a toy breaks is a pretty good lesson. Also worth remembering is that most kindergartners already have enough trinkets, toy dinos, rubber spiders, and other silly doodads stashed away in their bedroom hiding places. They really don't need any more junk.

But at some point, their interests and attention are going to shift from silly to serious. Hopefully, they always maintain some of their childlike innocence, even while beginning to identify a mature interest in a legitimate pastime.

Which brings us to this concept: When your grandchild gets serious about a hobby or sport, then you have permission to get serious about gifts related to that hobby or sport.

It's a two-part challenge for grandparents who want to be respectfully supportive. On the one hand, it's important that you *do not* invest a week's paycheck on a Dunlop Grand Slam racket or Miken Rain carbon fiber bat when your grandkid is seven years old. They won't appreciate it. They won't use it properly. They won't take care of it. And, most of all, that kind of investment puts a lot of pressure on everyone involved. Even if you can afford it, just don't.

The flip side of that idea is that—at the right time—go ahead and buy your grandson or granddaughter the best gosh darn bat, catcher's glove, tennis racket, turf shoes, climbing gear, microscope, telescope, art easel and oil paints, trumpet, fishing pole, bass guitar, pottery wheel, camera, or ice skates you can find.

In most of these examples, we're talking hundreds and hundreds of dollars. We're also talking about a once-in-a-lifetime gift.

Probably when the young recipient is not so young anymore. Maybe fifteen or sixteen years old. Or twenty. Or twenty-five. One rule of thumb might be to wait until they know—when they open it—exactly how big a deal it is. That sophomore catcher who just made the varsity team should squeal, "Ohmigosh, it's a Wilson 2021!" That's when you know you did it right.

Speaking from experience, here are a few more principles on investing in quality gear for your growing, enthusiastic, and focused grandchild.

If you're going to do the research and make the investment, it should probably be a version of that gear or instrument they can use for several years or well into their adulthood. Spending big bucks on ice skates your granddaughter outgrows in six months is a little excessive.

Involve your grandchild's parents in the decision. Yes, you would like to surprise them too. But if you're tuned into that young person's hopes and dreams, then they probably are as well. Their advice will be quite valuable regarding brands, sizes, styles, and many other factors. They might already have that same dream gift on layaway for their son or daughter's birthday. Even if it was their guidance that led you to the exact make and model, you can still take the credit. But please remember, like many of the actions you want to take as a grandparent, your own kids have veto power.

Finally, I apologize if this chapter makes you feel like you're attempting to buy your grandchildren's love. Actually, it's just the opposite. Your investment is saying, "Grandchild, I see how hard you're working. I see how you're setting goals. I'm proud of who you are and what you've already accomplished. I'm your greatest cheerleader. I share your dreams."

Make sure you also add, "No matter what, I promise to love you unconditionally."

Being an awesome grandparent does not require you to spend hundreds of dollars on your grandchildren. If you have a big family, that can add up real quick. But many men and women of retirement age have been scrimping and saving for years waiting for a rainy day or the right investment. What could possibly be more worthwhile? •

10
THE ADVANTAGE OF LIVING CLOSE

My folks never moved away. I don't think it was ever considered, even during the snowiest Chicago winter or hottest Chicago summer. The fact that they had eleven grandkids within 6 miles (10 km) may have had something to do with it.

I've seen firsthand the very real benefits of kids living near their grandparents. Applause doubles at most concerts, recitals, and soccer games. A big family showing up at events and supporting a young athlete or artist is a blessing that can't be overstated. The youngster may not say it, but they deeply appreciate it—at any and every age. On occasions when moms and dads can't be there, it's even more important when Grandma and/or Grandpa shows up in the bleachers or auditorium.

When grandparents live nearby, holiday travel plans are much, much easier. If those travel plans fall apart, there's no hard feelings because you can all get together the following week. Seats get saved on parade routes, for firework displays, at football games, and in church pews.

Emergencies are a little less urgent. Last-minute babysitters are (almost) always available. Emergency contact numbers are not neighbors, but grandparents.

Another benefit is that visits are generally shorter. Why is that good? Because no one "overstays their welcome." No one feels like they have to squeeze every drop of connection out of each visit. There are no dramatic tear-filled driveway good-byes because there's a high likelihood you'll see each other again in the next couple of weeks—or sooner. Whether you're visiting them or they're visiting you, there will come a time when it's quite clear the kids are getting cranky or Grandpa needs his nap. Deciding to make the short drive home is a no-brainer. There should be no hard feelings when someone—preferably an adult—says, "Let's call it a day."

The flip side of that idea is how living close opens the door to quick visits. At our house, even in the middle of a busy day, there's great joy when a daughter-in-law pulls into the driveway with a couple of grandkids to pick up or drop off a package, borrowed tool, or lost article of clothing. Kids jump out of the SUV, providing ten minutes of priceless hugs and chitchat. Living close provides a steady stream of serendipitous give-and-take. Lawns get mowed. Cookies get made. Life gets shared.

Let me be clear. I'm not suggesting you live *Everybody Loves Raymond* close. If you recall, the sitcom that aired on CBS from 1996 to 2005 featured aggressively meddlesome grandparents living right across the street from their son and his family. If you want additional insight on how *not* to be a grandparent, there are lessons in every episode.

In a later chapter, we'll kick around the benefits and challenges of three generations all living in the same home for a season. Which is another entire level of intimacy that can be quite rewarding for all involved.

All that to say, the benefits of living close are not guaranteed. The next short chapter offers some insight on why living a couple of states away—or even across the globe—can be the foundation for wonderful and rewarding intergenerational relationships. ●

Don't be surprised if becoming a grandparent finds you reevaluating many life decisions, including where you live, when you retire, and what people call you.

11

THE ADVANTAGE OF LIVING FAR AWAY

Sincere apologies if that last chapter made you feel a little sad. You may be one of the grandparents reading this book who only gets a chance to hug your grandkids—at most—two or three times per year. But take heart. There are plenty of strategies for effective long-distance grandparenting. And there are even *benefits* to your situation you may not have considered.

One idea to embrace is the practice of intentionality. Grandparents who live in the same town sometimes take their proximity for granted. Interactions with grandkids come and go and are not fully appreciated. In the course of an entire season, perhaps very few get-togethers are actually scheduled. Time with your grandchildren becomes hit or miss.

Conversely, when several hours of travel are required to see those growing kids, you will be much more intentional about making and executing plans. Purposefully arranging visits—coming or going—becomes part of the grandparenting experience. By definition, planning leads to thoughtful and meaningful time together. All three generations are in on the fun.

We're not suggesting that when Meemaw and Poppa come to town everyone drops everything to frantically make every minute count. But your arrival often means the entire family takes a day or two (or more) to focus on engaging activities, thoughtful meal preparation, and memorable benchmarks. Same thing is true when kids and grandkids visit your home. It's an event! Time is carefully carved out of everyone's calendar.

Joint vacations also become more creative and momentous. Coordinate calendars, pick a long weekend or an entire week, and

SPECIAL DELIVERIES

A splendid way to connect with your grandkids is having gifts from you show up on their doorstep. Online shopping makes that idea easier and cheaper than ever, and it's so rewarding you may even want to take advantage of this tactic even if you live in the same community. The post office and UPS are promoting new efforts to be more convenient. Amazon and almost all online vendors allow you to change the ship-to address and include gift receipts. Some even wrap the gift for you and allow you to write a personalized note. Also, there are local retailers and florists in the same zip code as your grandchildren who would love to make a delivery on your behalf.

let your imagination take over. Maybe meet at a location that has personal meaning to your family or pick a spot that's halfway between your homes. Whether it's a onetime gathering or an annual event, you'll be creating memories associated with a specific whereabouts. Because your time together is more precious, every member of the family will develop a personal memory bank of landmarks and milestones.

One of the obvious strategies for staying connected is Face-Time, Skype, or Zoom calls. Advancing technology has made face-to-face on-screen conversations second nature to anyone who has a smartphone or laptop. By the way, much better than scheduling a marathon video call every month would be brief unscheduled calls "just to check in" two or three times a week. Frequent visits are chattier and less awkward. If someone says, "Can't talk now," it's not a problem. Hanging up is never heart-wrenching because you're going to see those smiling faces again in a few days.

When your grandkids get their own phones, ask permission and then—judiciously—send an occasional text. Be warned, you can easily overdo this. But if you can find a common interest or develop a few inside jokes, you may deepen a lifelong connection with a grandchild that's the envy of all your friends. Again, stay positive and don't read too much into it if some of your texts aren't returned.

The US Postal Service is still making deliveries, and there's not a youngster alive who isn't thrilled with finding a letter or card with their name on it in their home mailbox. My grandson Judah lives just 10 miles (16 km) away, but we've become pen pals, of sorts, dropping notes and handmade booklets in the mail—which we'll both cherish forever. For the older grandkids, slip in an Andrew Jackson and suggest they take a friend out for ice cream, Starbucks, or a cold beverage. You might think a gift card is more personal, but trust me, teens prefer cash.

Birthdays, graduations, and other special occasions can still be celebrated from a distance. Put a card in the mail several days ahead of time. Call on the day of. Have a carefully chosen, nicely wrapped gift ready for the next time you see them in person—even if it's weeks away. Suddenly birthdays are not just a single day; they get celebrated over an extended period of time.

When shopping and remembering special days from a distance, it really is the thought that counts. If you know your grandchildren already have everything they need, then really it's just the excitement of being remembered that makes the most difference.

Because you see each other less frequently, it's important—and welcoming—to share lots of photos. Go ahead and send that photo of the squirrel in your birdfeeder or the rainbow at the beach. Insist you see a pic of your granddaughter's new haircut or the young athlete in their new uniform.

If you communicate in a lighthearted style—sending jokes and silly pics, sharing your own creative exploits—there's a much better chance they'll respond in kind.

Of course, much of this book contains strategies for personally engaging your grandchildren, which may seem like you're out of the loop and out of luck. But don't go there. Unleash your own creativity to incorporate ways to make that connection those young people sincerely need. Even from far away. ●

12

PAY FOR PIANO LESSONS

When grandparents pay for piano lessons, at least six things might happen. And they're all good.

FIRST—and most obvious—you're enabling that youngster to pursue a valuable and rewarding skill. If they enjoy it and keep at it, there's a high likelihood music will bring joy to their entire life.

SECOND, it's equally possible your grandchild will not master the piano. Maybe they give it a couple of years and decide it's not their thing. That's okay. Not every kid has the music gene. But during those weeks sitting on that piano bench, they'll develop a deeper appreciation for music and musicians.

THIRD, you're supporting the arts. Quite literally, you're putting money in the pocket of a piano teacher, ensuring that the world has more music. That's a welcome gift to humanity.

FOURTH, you're helping balance your son or daughter's budget. All families go through periods when money is tight. When cuts are being considered, piano lessons for the kids are a line item that may seem nonessential. Since you're footing the bill, that's no longer a question. Plus, some young parents may be a little too proud to ask for financial help, but they will say yes to grandparents paying for music lessons.

FIFTH, through your generosity you have earned permission to say, "Hey, Cole, how's the piano going?" Then, if there's a piano nearby, you might even say, "Play me a tune. Anything you want. Even if it's something you're working on that's not quite polished." Chances are your request will be honored. By the way, that mini-concert will also be a gift to the pianist's parents. When Grandma or Grandpa ask, there's a better chance they'll sit down at the piano than when Mom or Dad asks. When my own kids were first learning to play, it was a request from Papa that allowed me to hear their best work.

SIXTH, let's imagine music becomes a significant and passionate part of their life. You can take some of the credit! When they get a public acknowledgment from the middle-school band director, scholarship to Juilliard, recording contract, or standing ovation at Carnegie Hall, your heart will swell with pride. They may even mention your love and encouragement in their Grammy Award acceptance speech. (Did you ever wonder why they call it a "Grammy"?)

Even if you can't swing the cost of piano lessons—which could be a couple hundred bucks a month—support of your grandchildren's artistic activities should be an ongoing endeavor. Whether it's classical music, techno, dance, sculpting, painting, storytelling, slam poetry, photography, filmmaking, podcasting, new media, or whatever, make sure their exhibits and performances are on your calendar. Attend every one you can, and if you can't make it, insist on a full report and video, if possible.

An intergenerational connection through the arts can be a blast and a blessing. Believe me, it's a memorable experience when grandparents grab a corner table at a brew pub to watch their grandson's band play a raucous set of covers and original tunes. I've seen it firsthand. Sometimes—between songs—Mimi and Papa even get a shout-out from the lead singer. ●

Music connects generations. Ever wonder why teenagers know the lyrics to songs their grandparents grew up with?

13

DON'T APOLOGIZE FOR YOUR GENERATION

A warning for grandparents: As you ease past middle age, you will find yourself partaking in activities that earn you a bit of mocking from the next one or two generations. Even from those grandkids who love you so much.

When you do stuff that's considered "ancient history," it's reasonable to expect a certain amount of eye-rolling and verbal derision. Most of their boorish words are good-natured, but not all of them.

Some may hurt a bit. My recommendation is to double down on who you are and what you believe. Recommit to being the wonderful, bullheaded, unshakable hero that you are. Proudly stand up for your generation. Don't compromise your beliefs. Be empowered by your life experience.

Allow me to list some of those activities you cherish. Activities that were effective life strategies long before your grandkids and even your kids were born. Some you may have learned from your own grandparents. Frankly, there's no reason to stop now.

READING A NEWSPAPER Never apologize for reading an actual full-length article printed with real ink (or online) written by a real-life reporter who earned a four-year degree in journalism.

Your children and any older grandchildren think they are keeping up on world events by viewing tweets, texts, and posts while stopped at a red light and glancing down at their phones. Not surprisingly, their opinions formed on minimal information are almost never in sync with your well-thought-out assessment of how the world should work. Your grandchildren need you to keep reading those newspapers.

WRITING IN CURSIVE Never apologize for writing an entire word without lifting your pen or pencil off the paper. It's faster. It's prettier. And you've earned the right. You practiced cursive for hours in second and third grade, dragging a pencil as big as a horse's leg across that fibrous paper with the green tint and alternating rows of straight lines and dotted lines. You could only fit maybe seven or eight words on each sheet, but they were remarkably legible.

When the upcoming generation picks up a pencil, they only know how to print and even get angry when they can't read your writing. Maybe we should think of cursive as a secret code to use with other grandparents.

PUTTING WEIRD STUFF IN JELL-O Never apologize for adding shredded carrots, mandarin oranges, or pineapple rings to lime Jell-O. If your offspring at the table grimace or make rude comments, it's their loss. That just means there's more for those who appreciate the finer things in life.

When you hear disparaging words about any item on your menu, inform those ungrateful whiners how lucky they are not to have to eat crusty tuna surprise, mushy canned asparagus, breaded Spam, or wieneroni casserole. How did we survive that?

DRINKING BLACK COFFEE Never apologize for how you order coffee. After all, a good strong cup of coffee is the only way you survived mornings with those little darlings who now mock you for drinking black coffee. Do not feel any obligation to order something ridiculous like a "grande half-caf triple skinny extra hot caramel latte." Also, let's be clear. It's perfectly fine to say "large" instead of "venti." Your barista will know what you mean.

The list goes on. What are other things grandparents do but our kids and grandkids don't? Leaving voicemails, peeling apples, wallpapering, doing crossword puzzles, decorating with throw pillows, separating laundry, ironing, talking to strangers on planes, buying real furniture, sending postcards, and keeping our landline. Is any of that wrong?

If your children and grandchildren choose to mock you in a spirit of love, joy, and camaraderie, then let them have their fun. You might feel the urge, but there's no reason to mock them back for their copious amount of selfies, torn blue jeans, fixation on craft beer, sense of entitlement, dependence on their phones, and so many more irritating quirks and preferences. Even though they started it, they might not appreciate your joke!

Last thought on the matter: If you are ever truly verbally attacked because of the supposed mess our generation has made of the world, feel free to respond by listing some of our notable contributions that are often taken for granted. That includes information technology, human rights, globalism, life-saving health care advancements, space exploration, environmental awareness, *SNL*, NPR, rock and roll, disposable diapers, pet rocks, the spork, and so much more. ●

Generations will always see things differently. It's the circle of life and love.

14

MAKE SURE YOU'RE MISSED

I didn't cry at my grandfather's funeral. He was seventy-eight. I was a junior in college.

I grew up in the Chicago suburbs, about two hours from where Nana and Grandpa Fritz lived, and I probably saw them four or five times a year. My family would drive up to Racine, Wisconsin, for Christmas, Thanksgiving, and Easter. Occasionally, they would drive down, but the visits were short and not memorable. Maybe they weren't comfortable spending the night. Maybe they had better things to do.

Doing the math, over my first twenty years of life, I would have had about a hundred chances to interact with my father's parents. All the short visits, at our house or theirs, were stiff and pretty much uncomfortable. But every year in early August we would spend an entire week with them up at Pine Lake in northern Wisconsin. Those days were not awkwardly stiff at all—they were filled with catching fish, gutting fish, eating fish, swimming, hiking, playing family-friendly games, and sitting around the fireplace in the big cabin that held more than a dozen members of my extended family. All solid memories.

Being "Up North" for an entire week with Nana and Grandpa Fritz gave me a taste of what a relationship between kids and grandparents could be. But only a taste. That wonderful annual experience on the lake still did not create enough closeness to stir any true depth of feeling for Grandpa Fritz when he passed away. I didn't really know the man. And vice versa. At the time, I didn't realize what I had missed. I also will never know whether Grandpa Fritz had any regrets.

Standing in dramatic contrast is the wake and funeral service of my own father about eight years ago. In front of a roomful of mourners, my four sons each spent a few minutes sharing heartfelt personal memories of time spent with Papa. The words spoken by Alec, Randall, Max, and Isaac all reflected the intimate relationship they had with my dad, of which even I was jealous. The funeral parlor and church overflowed with laughter and weeping. While they spoke, all four young men had to stop more than once to gather their composure and brush back streaming tears. It was a beautiful thing. It was a tribute to what the relationship between grandparents and grandkids can be.

How do relationships like that happen? Well, it's not by accident. Looking back, I can identify specific decisions my parents made that opened the door to the bond they had with my kids. But I also realized that much of it is a result of grandparents just being there. Making time. Showering grandchildren not with cash and gifts but with love and attention.

It's not easy to put into words, but allow me to try anyway. The cross-generational connection between you and your grandkids might be the only human relationship in which you can find joy simply in who *they* are and who *you* are. Lean into that feeling. Don't be so caught up in the scheduling, discipline, and deliberation that you miss out on the wonder. The wonder of grandparenting. ●

15

WORTHWHILE WARNINGS

This book is filled with ideas grandparents can do—events, projects, outings, games, gifts, words, and strategies that bring joy, connect generations, and make memories. However, this chapter does the opposite. Let's call it twenty things *not* to do.

Some of these actions to be avoided may not apply to your particular family. Some are mere minor missteps. Some are way worse. The list really should be self-explanatory. If you're not sure, ask your grandchildren's mom and dad. I promise they will have opinions.

PLEASE DON'T...

1. Post photos of your grandkids on social media without permission.

2. Indulge the grandkids with unlimited junk food.

3. Offer ancient and outdated parenting advice.

4. Grimace when the parents announce the name of the new baby.

5. Let the grandkids get away with murder.

6. Take a young grandchild to get their hair cut or ears pierced. Or any of life's firsts.

7. Ignore the parents' dietary instructions for the children.

8. Hint, suggest, or demand the parents give you another grandchild.

9. Treat grandsons differently than granddaughters.

10. Ignore the potty-training regimen established by Mom and Dad.

11. Permit grandchildren to watch forbidden, graphic, or scary stuff.

Hooray for

12. Teach the grandchildren naughty and insensitive words—even inadvertently.

13. Overlook the car seat mandate.

14. Serve alcohol or weed to your underage grandkids. Or overserve yourself while they are in your care.

15. Neglect new research regarding sleeping and child safety.

16. Comment negatively on your grandchild's weight, acne, attention span, clothing choices, prescriptions, or other issues that Mom and Dad are already aware of.

17. Bad-mouth relatives (especially your grandchild's other grandparents!).

18. Initiate conversations about death, religion, or sex with your grandchildren.

19. Interrogate your grandchildren about what's up with their mom and dad.

20. Give a drum kit, trampoline, iPhone, pet, or some other overwhelming gift without permission.

A little common sense should help you avoid all these blunders. Or maybe this list doesn't sit well with you. Do you regularly find yourself on a completely different page than your grandchildren's parents? Take heart; you're not alone and your instincts are probably exactly right. Still, unless it's cruel or physically dangerous, Mom and Dad's rules and expectations take precedence over Grandma and Grandpa's.

On the other hand, your grandchild's parents may be struggling in their own way with many of the issues reflected above. You might be the exact right sounding board for your son, daughter, son-in-law, or daughter-in-law. In your own way, let them know they can come to you for nonjudgmental advice on health issues, prescription meds, religious education, childhood obesity, eating disorders, keeping teenagers safe, and other sensitive areas. Once they broach the topic, then feel free to deliver humble wisdom, promising to keep it confidential.

Just to confirm, there are things you may think are no big deal, but might be just about unforgivable to your kid and their spouse. The best (or worst) example might be taking your toddler grandson on his first trip to the barber for a buzz cut of his beautiful curly hair. Yikes! ●

MAKE LIFE SAFER AND EASIER

The first time you volunteer to watch a crawling grandbaby in your home, the memories will come flooding back. Toddlers always head right for electric outlets, steep staircases, window blind cords, and cabinets with cleaning supplies. The difference is that this time they're faster and you're slower. If you watch toddlers more than a couple of times a year, installing baby gates and babyproofing a few rooms in your home is probably worth the time and effort. Purchasing and installing a booster seat for your own car is an even better idea. Wrestling a child safety seat from one car to another is a nightmare you will want to avoid.

Grandparenting instincts are 98 percent exactly right. Be wary of that 2 percent.

16

PROBLEM- SOLVING AT THE PARK

Parents have a lot on their plate. And it's inescapable. Even if a mom or dad relinquishes to their child's request to go to the playground, their myriad responsibilities are never far from their mind. In some ways, today's parents never allow themselves to fully engage with their children.

You've seen the scene many times. A youngster is climbing, hanging, swinging, spinning, leaping, and monkeying all over a giant colorful plastic jungle gym. Meanwhile, Mom or Dad is sitting or standing just off to the side of the play area, phone in hand, texting, talking, or checking emails. That might seem like a tragically poor choice, but I hope you'll join me in refraining from making any kind of judgment. The digital communication could be urgent and that parent really should get all kinds of bonus points just for making it to the park.

Overall, that scene is a parenting victory. Their kid is getting some exercise, testing their physical skills, and enjoying themselves. But I can't help but wonder whether a child's visit to that giant playground with an adult who had a little more time and a few less distractions might yield an even grander experience.

That's where grandparents come in. Maybe our stamina and flexibility have diminished, but we can make up for it by offering undivided attention to something as commonplace as a visit to the playground. With any luck, we could even turn it into a multi-faceted learning experience connecting physical activity with creativity and mental acuity. A few months ago, this revelation came to me on a fairly brief—maybe twenty-minute—adventure with my grandson Jackson on a wonderfully engaging playground apparatus in our hometown.

It was spring and right away I could tell the seven-year-old had developed new muscle and coordination over the winter. Especially impressive was his ability to tirelessly maneuver hand over hand along a long set of curvy monkey bars. One of the features of the jungle gym was an iron wheel on a spinning axle that looked very much like a small steering wheel facing the ground. Older kids could jump, hang from that wheel, and use their body torque to spin in a circle. The inviting device was just out of Jackson's reach. He could jump high enough to touch it, but couldn't quite grab hold.

After several attempts, the obvious next step was for Chief—that's me—to lift him so that he could grab that wheel and give it a whirl. We could have stopped with that small achievement, but here's where the wisdom of Jackson's grandfather revealed itself.

I asked the question, "Hey, Jack, what are other ways you might grab hold of that wheel?" As I was formulating some solutions, Jackson was doubling down on his own physical efforts. As only a seven-year-old boy can do, he squatted low in an effort to jump higher. Then he tried backing up to get a running start. He jumped, reaching with one hand. He tried several quick jumps in succession. Each time he was just millimeters short of securing a grip.

With Jackson, I teased out some other possible solutions. Could we lower the wheel? No. Could we get springier sneakers? Maybe. On his own, Jack tried to jump from a nearby platform, but it was too far away. Then through trial and error and some additional creative brainstorming, we formulated four methods for Jackson to reach that wheel that actually worked. Can you guess what they were?

One was to scrape together a small mound of woodchips to give Jackson a slightly higher elevation from which to jump. It worked and he proudly hung on and spun.

Another was to take off his sweatshirt. We weren't sure whether the weight was limiting his leap or whether his arm movement was restricted by the sweatshirt. In any case, that was one more method for gaining that extra inch he needed to reach the wheel.

The third method—which has not yet been proven but will certainly work—was patience. I suggested we could simply come back to the playground later that summer. He would surely keep growing and getting stronger and, by then, that jump and grab would be "a cinch." To his credit, Jackson nodded his head, acknowledging that he grasped the concept.

Interestingly, that idea of "someday" inspired him to make one more focused try that day. Even though his first twenty jumps were short, that next attempt was successful. Under identical conditions, he then found himself routinely able to reach the wheel. Even while wearing his sweatshirt and leaping from flat woodchips. What was the difference? We decided it was a combination of experience, tenacity, and confidence. Once he experienced gripping the wheel, it morphed from impossible to possible. That's quite a lesson.

Hooray for

What's the takeaway for grandparents? First, have patience and carve out creative playtime with your grandkids that Mom and Dad might not always have.

Second, get in the habit of asking open-ended questions: How can we do this? What are other options? What resources do we have? What's the real goal?

Third, take any chance you get to engage your grandchildren in connecting physical and mental activities. Linking mind and body develops cognitive connections in their brains that will serve them well for years to come, whether they're dancing ballet, memorizing a script, pole vaulting, welding an I beam, or arguing a case in court.

Fourth, take that little one you love so much to a playground ASAP. •

Even more rewarding than answering a young person's questions is questioning their answers.

17

LEAVING THE LIGHT ON

Adult children moving back home has become much more routine than it was for my generation. In a recent five-year period, the number of twenty-five- to thirty-four-year-olds in the United States living with their parents increased by nearly one million. According to a 2020 article in the *Atlantic*, "The New Boomerang Kids Could Change American Views of Living at Home," the trend continues.

There's an excellent chance your own kids have been part of the boomerang generation. They moved out . . . and then moved back in. Maybe it was after graduation or after a breakup or job loss. In many cases, it was a wise financial decision. They were in their early or mid-twenties, looked at Mom and Dad's big house, realized their old room was still empty, and saw a chance to pay off college loans or save for their own place.

Initially the term *boomerang generation* was tossed around like a disparaging slam. It was a mocking reference to young people who "couldn't survive in the real world," but that's not really the case. For many families, adult kids moving home worked out well. (Full disclosure, three of our five kids lived with Rita and me after college, and it was a great season of connecting with them as adults. Sitting around our kitchen table, we saw those hopes and dreams we talked about back when they were in high school actually begin to blossom. Rita and I are now back to having an empty nest.)

What does that have to do with grandparenting? Well, it's not just singles who are boomeranging home. Couples—with babies—are also temporarily moving in with their parents for similar reasons. And it's fantastic. (Or can be.)

If your son or daughter—maybe the one with the new grandbaby who gave you this book—comes to you with a plan that involves temporary housing, listen carefully. And try to say yes. They wouldn't come to you unless they had thought it through, and their reasoning very well may be solid.

The turn of events with our middle child and his family is a perfect example. After their first son was starting to crawl, Max and his young wife, Megan, began seriously house hunting. The lease on their townhouse rental was up and their landlord couldn't give them the option to rent month to month, which meant they needed to find temporary housing. When Max asked if they could move into the big room in the upstairs corner of our house, we didn't even hesitate. It was a memorable and rollicking six months.

During the COVID pandemic, my youngest son, Isaac, found himself in a similar situation while working for a national brand computer company. He and his wife, Kaitlin, had already sold their house in the Nashville area but needed a place to stay while waiting for Isaac's new sales territory assignment. With two kids and another on the way, they moved in with Kaitlin's parents for several months. Again, it worked out to everyone's advantage, creating new memories and new appreciation for the love, commitment, and benefit of family.

Those two experiences—as well as stories collected from dozens of other families—suggest that keeping the light on for young families in transition is more than just an experience to endure. It's an experience to pursue.

So I recommend you put it out there. If there's space in your house, let your son or daughter know that you would welcome their family with open arms, especially if there's a transition plan in place. Then enter into that arrangement with both optimism and a reality check. Assume it's going to be amusing and memorable. But also know that you will most assuredly both have to make some, well, adjustments. Questions will come up: What's on TV? Who ate my leftovers? Who's picking up/paying for the pizza? Can you move your car? Are you going to church with us? Who used all the hot water? Have you seen my gray sweatshirt? What's this stain on the couch?

Of course, the younger couple freeloading at their folks' place should show great appreciation and be the most flexible. But the homeowner should not be surprised when a gallon of milk doesn't last a week or the utility bill is a bit higher.

A handful of reasonable people of differing generations who love and respect each other should be able to survive a season or two together under the same roof. Memories will be made, guaranteed. The goal is for the laughter to overshadow the eye rolls. ●

It's not a bad thing when your grown kids think of home as home.

18
TELL YOUR STORY

Long after you're gone, you want your grandkids to remember you. Not just from those years during which you were their grand-parent. You want them to understand who you were *back in your tender years*. Back when you were their age. Or when you were just starting out and chasing a dream. When you were daring new conquests and taking on the world, sometimes having to dust yourself off, learn from your mistakes, dig deep, and try again.

The story of your awakening just might provoke them to dream their own dreams and risk their own risks. That's right. Your legacy—even after you're gone—can inspire future generations to greatness. A middle schooler may not want to listen to their parents drone on and on about "When I was your age . . ." But they will eagerly listen to long-lost tales from Grandma and Grandpa.

Sure, you're hesitant. You may be worried about boring them. You may think the lessons you learned decades ago don't apply to today's busier, louder, tech-centric world. Memories of your youth may be swirling in a fog that makes them seem irretrievable. You may think your story doesn't amount to much.

Think again. You learned—and can reinforce—lessons that are applicable and valuable to every generation. How to persevere through disappointments. How to find joy in the moment. How to earn your keep. How to get along with people who are different than you. How to make friends. How the best things in life are free. How to stand up for yourself. How to stand up for the less fortunate. How to see the big picture.

If you don't remember how you learned those life lessons, let's get specific. Here are twelve questions that should trigger memories worth sharing.

1. What was unusual about the town or neighborhood in which you grew up?

2. Who was your best friend at every age? How did you meet? Are you still friends?

3. Did you have a favorite hangout, such as a rec center, park, shopping mall, forest, or vacant lot?

4. Were you ever rushed to the hospital, sent to the principal's office, or stopped by a cop?

5. What was your first job? Best job? Worst job?

6. Did you have a nickname? What was your reputation?

7. What was your favorite subject in school? What did you want to be when you grew up?

8. What was your favorite book, movie, television show, music group, or board game?

9. What was your best or worst road trip or vacation?

10. Who was your first boyfriend or girlfriend? How did you meet? When was your first kiss?

11. What is your biggest disappointment or regret? Did you ever lose a friend over something stupid?

12. What's something you did that you never told your parents about?

After that flood of memories, I hope you see that you have much to share. What's more, you may be thinking, *I wish I knew more about my own grandparents*. Let that thought and the love for your grandkids spur you into a long season of memory sharing.

Of course, if you talk about failures, make sure you talk about how you overcame them with flying colors. If you talk about horrid experiences, confirm that you survived and can now laugh about them. If you talk about friendships, let your grandkids know that to get a friend you have to be a friend. When talking about your early romances, emphasize the value you discovered in cherish-ing relationships and fostering mutual respect.

All the while, don't be too obvious, deliberate, or preachy when delivering life lessons. Just tell your story and you'll find the truths, warnings, and wisdom flow naturally and, often, unexpectedly. •

Your grandkids may not sit at your feet and ask to hear your life story, but they yearn for that connection.

19

TELL YOUR GRAND-PARENTS' STORY

Pondering the previous chapter, you may have realized—with a bit of regret—that you don't know much about your own grandma and grandpa.

That tug on your heart should inspire you to proactively chronicle your story to your own grandchildren. As suggested in the last chapter, start with your story. Include plenty of anecdotes about your own children—your grandchildren's parents, aunts, and uncles—and then dig deeper into family lore. Any memories or anecdotes you have about your own parents and grandparents should also be passed along to that upcoming generation. Don't be surprised if you find yourself spinning yarns dating back a century or more! The benefits are wonderfully rewarding.

Your twelve-year-old granddaughter never met her great-great-grandparents. But you could be the one to describe the scene of how they fell in love at first sight at Coney Island. Then how they died just a few days apart sixty years later. That would help her imagine meeting her own perfect partner someday.

Tell your nine-year-old grandson about how his great-great-grandfather shoveled coal on a steamship, sold encyclopedias door-to-door, or stormed the beaches of Normandy on D-Day. That helps instill a work ethic and patriotism that every kid needs.

Describe the two-bedroom apartment your grandma lived in with her mother, father, and five siblings. That should stop any complaining about the size of their closet or having to share a bathroom.

Tell your teenage grandkids about the firsts in your family history. The first to come to America. The first to gain citizenship or vote. The first to graduate college. The first to leave the family business for other pursuits. The first to own their own home. You just might help them become pioneers themselves.

Tell about the stuff your predecessors had to overcome. Racial discrimination. Religious persecution. The Great Depression. Rationing during World War II. Japanese internment camps. Polio, measles, smallpox. Don't forget—as legend has it—how your grandparents had to walk to school uphill both ways in the snow. Even worse, they only had 16-inch (41 cm) black-and-white televisions with a pitiful three channels. Besides that, they suffered through the trauma of having to fold road maps and remember phone numbers.

In all seriousness, your tales may reach back through history and introduce your grandkids to a world they can only imagine. One friend, Matthew, told me his grandfather walked the city streets with a long pole every night at dusk to light gas streetlamps. My friend Bernie told me his grandfather met his grandmother when—working as a bellhop—he carried her trunk off a stagecoach.

The year I was born, my mom's parents moved to Albuquerque, New Mexico, because my grandfather had been recruited for a secret government job. That was 1957, and the nuclear arms race was coming of age. No one in the family, not even Grandma, knew what Orlando Mauel did. Fifteen years earlier, the supersecret lab at nearby Los Alamos had been ground zero for research for the Manhattan Project, the Allied effort to produce the atomic weapons that effectively ended World War II. Family lore suggests that Grandpa Mauel worked at Sandia National Laboratories, a branch of Los Alamos.

One more reason you need to follow the advice of this chapter is that passing on family stories often skips generations. There may be stories parents don't share with their own children for any number of reasons, but with grandchildren they finally feel comfortable or have the time to put those memories into words.

One final example stands out. My father, part of the greatest generation, served in the US Army at the end of World War II. Growing up, I never heard stories of his experiences in the Pacific. But I'll never forget looking out the kitchen window into the side yard of my parents' home and seeing my dad and my eleven-year-old daughter in deep conversation. Later I asked Rae Anne what they were talking about. Matter-of-factly, she said, "Oh, Papa was just telling me about his days in the army." •

20
PUT HISTORY IN CONTEXT

Even after reading the last two chapters, you may not realize what a gift it is to commingle your own family history with world and national history. Be assured, making those connections can have a profound impact on your grandchildren's lives.

Your grandkids (and their parents, for that matter) never knew a time when cell phones and computers didn't exist. They can access information faster than any generation that ever lived. But, unless they are real students of history, your children and their children have little sense about when and why things happened.

Sure, today's middle schoolers may have heard about 9/11, Pearl Harbor, Watergate, and the Gettysburg Address. They vaguely recognize the names Thomas Edison, Neil Armstrong, Johannes

Gutenberg, and Steve Jobs. But they probably can't place them in the context of history. They certainly couldn't confirm that Edison was working on perfecting the incandescent light bulb about twenty years after the Civil War. Or that Pearl Harbor and 9/11 were sixty years apart. Or that Jobs began his work a half millennium after Gutenberg.

Many of the grandparents reading this book have some recollection of Neil Armstrong walking on the moon. You probably also could give a little historical context to the civil rights movement, Woodstock, the first PCs, the Space Shuttle *Challenger*, the fall of the Berlin Wall, the Columbine shooting, and the Y2K panic. It's all part of your life, but it's "history" to your grandchildren. Can you see how investing in a walk down memory lane recalling the real-life events in your head would be much more valuable to your grandchildren than just about anything else they might be doing this weekend?

You've seen firsthand the continual evolution in technology, geopolitics, social revolution, exploration, and subsequent career options. Pass on that concept, and your grandchildren will realize new ideas and new opportunities are constantly surfacing. As they seek their place in this world, many children can't imagine where they're going to fit. You can help them avoid frustration or depression by giving them a vision for a changing world that will present all kinds of unforeseen life choices. Your look back at history gives them motivation and a reason to pursue experience and wisdom for the future.

Talking about the experiences of you, your parents, and your grandparents can help your grandchild frame the entire twentieth century in a way that no history book could possibly do. What's more, your perspective will be free of the many political

IF YOU DON'T TELL YOUR FAMILY STORIES, WHO WILL?

Through storytelling or sketching out the family tree, see if you can paint an imaginative picture of your recent ancestors and their place in history. Include names, dates, cities, and occupations, but don't worry if some of the facts are a little fuzzy. Maybe start with how your parents experienced the growing impact of television and the threat of the Cold War. Depending on your family history, your grandparents may have lived through the Great Depression and World War II and their parents—the great-great-grandparents of your grandkids—probably were the first in your family to flip on a light switch or see an airplane fly overhead. That generation survived the Spanish flu; today's generation survived COVID-19. A lot can happen in a century, give or take a decade or two.

Not sure which world events your parents and grandparents endured? Some online research will help you make a historical connection for the sake of your grandkids. And you might learn something too!

and social agendas that are found in classrooms, textbooks, and online resources.

Now you don't want to be that grandma or grandpa always talking about the "good old days" or whining about how easy life is for millennials or Gen Z. When you initiate a conversation about history, frame it in the context of a conversation. Become storytellers and secret keepers. Discern what's important to each of your grandchildren. Weave their discoveries, curiosities, and desires into the stories you tell.

Think of this assignment as giving them the gift of perspective. Helping them see how generational and historical connections are part of life will help your grandkids find their sweet spot.

Don't forget that even as you affirm culture and technology will change over time, you should also confirm that some things *don't* change. Such as the value of character traits like kindness, curiosity, personal discipline, respect, and the courage to do the right thing. The miracle of birth, the wonder of nature, and the responsibility to use our gifts wisely.

Also, let your grandchildren know that while the past can't be changed, it doesn't have to define you or limit your capabilities. Mistakes or missed opportunities can be overcome and even serve as learning experiences to make you stronger. Finally, assure your grandchildren that your unconditional love will never change. •

*Grandparents
are living
history books.*

21

MAYBE SHARE THEIR INHERITANCE EARLY

If you have a bit of a nest egg and are planning on leaving a modest or even sizable inheritance to your children after you die, I invite you to consider this scenario.

Out of the blue, bring your children together and—after a short speech—hand them each a check for an amount that makes them gasp. Just to be clear: You are not buying their affection, but you are definitely going to get some extra hugs and words of appreciation. Pretty cool, right?

In many cases, that financial windfall will come at the exact right time for your son or daughter trying to raise their own family. You remember those days, right? For most young families, it's surprising how expenses—housing, food, clothing, activities, emergencies, insurance, schooling, transportation—add up so quickly. Budgets are broken. Moms and dads are having to say no to their kids. Spouses argue about nickels and dimes. Vacations are out of the question.

Even if your children are solidly employed and good stewards of their money, they will very likely endure seasons of life when their income doesn't quite match their outgo.

What might your financial gift mean? If they just added a new baby, maybe Mom or Dad can stay home for a few extra months to give that newborn some more snuggles. Maybe one of those young parents can quit their second part-time job, which helps the family spend more quality time together.

If their children are involved in extracurricular activities, maybe they can invest in slightly better equipment, tools, or instruments. Or pay for lessons or coaching that make all the difference to your grandchild's success.

It's possible tight budgets have led them to delay some legitimate necessities: Braces for their kid's teeth. Serious household repairs. Hiring an exterminator. Replacing an unsafe car. Life-changing

THIS GOOD IDEA COMES WITH A FEW RELEVANT WARNINGS

WARNING #1: Sharing your nest egg early is *not* a suggested option for many grandparents. Your future cost of living and medical needs are uncertain. Your financial portfolio goes through highs and lows, leaving too many questions. A better option may be to maintain control over 100 percent of your own assets, so you don't become a burden to your children later on. That's okay. You can set aside this chapter.

WARNING #2: You cannot tell them what to do with that money. Once you give it, it's theirs. If you think you'll be frustrated or angry with their frivolous or wasteful purchase, don't even open this door.

WARNING #3: If you have more than one child, you really need to give the same amount to each of them. Yes, one family needs it more. Yes, one family has more kids than the other. Yes, one family is less responsible with money. But know this: If you give more or less to one family, you're initiating a feud between siblings.

WARNING #4: Be very clear that this is a onetime gift. If they think there's more coming, you may be setting them up for financial catastrophe. One well-meaning older couple gave out substantial checks to their three adult children for four Christmases in a row. Imagine the expectations and devastation on that fifth Christmas, when the money was gone.

WARNING #5: Beware of tax implications. Actually, every aspect of this topic should be scrutinized with your accountant and financial advisor.

therapy for one of your grandkids. You may never know what financial worries have been keeping them up at night.

Maybe your gift allows the family to finally take a much-needed relaxing and/or educational vacation. (Perhaps inviting you to come along!)

Maybe there's an unspoken dream your son, daughter, son-in-law, or daughter-in-law has been hoping to chase, but they just couldn't take a break from their career. Your generosity might give them the gift of time and make all the difference, launching them into a new world of creativity, joy, and long-lasting financial freedom. That's a legacy you can watch blossom that satisfies the soul.

You never know what your children have been imagining or what's keeping them up at night. Paying off burdensome college loans. Installing a swimming pool. Taking in a foster child. Moving out of a challenging neighborhood. Adding a three-season room. Buying a pony.

Are you starting to see the power and impact of providing them with an early inheritance? Truth be told, you will probably be totally surprised at what they do with that money. It might all go into savings. It might just help them breathe easier.

Dare I say, this is a new concept for most grandparents, and you need to carefully weigh the cost and benefits before cutting those checks. For some, this idea may be frustrating to consider because you think it's just not possible. Still, reviewing this chapter, you'll see that no dollar values were mentioned. That suggests that any amount could be a surprising, much-appreciated financial windfall of sorts.

Finally, never forget the most valuable inheritance you can leave is your own example of integrity, faith, and love. ●

22

STEER CLEAR OF BUYING THEIR LOVE

If your relationship with your children and grandchildren is mostly about money, then you've missed the entire point of grandparenting. But you knew that, right?

The previous chapter regarding offering your heirs an early inheritance made it clear that giving away money is a potentially dangerous proposition. Adult sibling relationships have been obliterated over surprisingly small amounts of money.

But what about financial gifts given directly to grandchildren? Isn't that a long-standing sacred rite of passage . . . and even an obligation? Don't all grandparents slip a silver dollar or a five-spot to a grandchild occasionally? Personally, I think that's okay. A token financial gift falls in the same gray area as taking a grandchild out for ice cream. It's not special treatment; it's just part of the adventure of the day. Still, be careful and don't get carried away. Playing favorites can put you on thin ice with moms, dads, uncles, aunts, and so on.

As for big fat checks and bills of larger denominations? Probably save those for special occasions. Who can argue with the wonderful tradition of getting a significant monetary congratulations from grandparents at graduations, weddings, and religious ceremonies like confirmations and bar and bat mitzvahs?

Well, hold on now. Here's something that may not have occurred to you. What about that grandchild who drops out of school to go into the trades or military? What about the one grandchild who chooses not to get married? Or isn't involved in their church or temple?

What are you saying about what's important if you leave them out? You certainly don't want your generosity (and love) contingent on their life choices, right?

It's tempting for grandparents to use financial gifts as a sort of bribery to advance an agenda. But don't overlook the possible repercussions. Know that it doesn't take much—just a few dollars here or there—to cause dissension among all those young people who mean so much to you.

Another challenge surfaces when financial rewards are based on performance. Ten dollars for As on report cards. Fifty dollars for reading a book. Two hundred dollars if you come for an afternoon visit. A thousand dollars for quitting smoking. Those are all good things for your grandkids to do. But what about the grandchild who gets Bs in much more challenging college prep classes? Or lives too far away to visit? Or has dyslexia? Or doesn't smoke?

Grandma and Grandpa, just make sure you think it through. There's a good chance that some of your grandkids are already feeling left behind or out of the loop. It's natural to reward grandchildren when they get applause and accolades for successes. But it's worth the effort to avoid making siblings and cousins envious in the process. Also, be consistent with dollar amounts for siblings and cousins who achieve identical milestones.

Your endorsement with words or gifts means so much. To make the most of it, you'll want to talk over gift-giving occasions and dollar amounts with your own children. Simply let them know what you're hoping to achieve. Be the grandparents who unite the family rather than cause strife. ●

A wise grandparent treats every grandchild differently. And the same.

23
A SUMMER MONTH AT NANA'S

When he was a boy, my friend Mitch would spend a month every summer at Nana's house in southern Indiana. An entire month. With his sister and two older brothers. Can you imagine?

For more than ten summers, the town of Scottsburg, just a half hour north of the Kentucky state line, became a second home of sorts to those four growing kids. Mitch and his siblings knew their way around town and had a gaggle of friends they looked forward to hanging out with year after year.

Mitch vividly remembers a ceremony of sorts that Nana held the first day of their annual arrival. She would save her pocket change all year in a Hills Bros. coffee can, which she dumped out on the rug in her living room. The four kids would divide the coins evenly and that would be their spending money for the month. Decades later, Mitch can't remember how much it was, but he insists, "It was a lot!"

Also on the first or second day of their arrival, Mitch remembered, "Nana would march all four of us to the general store on Main Street for a new pair of blue jeans." That would be their uniform for the month.

At first, Mitch and his sister and brothers would hang out as a pack, but rekindled summer friendships—and maybe even a young romance—would soon have the siblings going on their own adventures this way and that. They rationed their coffee can money on things they didn't need at the local five-and-dime and on cherry Cokes and sundaes at the drugstore soda fountain. Reflecting back, Mitch said the entire experience was eerily similar to Andy Griffith's fictitious Mayberry.

At the time, Mitch remembered thinking that his parents were being extraordinarily generous allowing all four of them to be away from home for such a long period of time. He laughs now, realizing they were "glad to be rid of us for the month."

As for Nana, it was the highlight of her year. Grandpa had passed before Mitch was born. The four kids were happy to do a little lawn mowing, minor upkeep, light kitchen duty, and so on. Nothing burdensome at all. Nana was a nurse, well-loved in the community, and always ready with a story about her grandchildren. She still worked her hospital shifts during that very special month, but she knew the kids would be fine. It was Scottsburg, after all. Everyone watched out for each other.

Even as Mitch described Nana's big old house not far from downtown, he realized that she didn't own it. It was a rental—the servants' quarters for an even bigger house on the same piece of property. As can happen with memories from our youth, the realities blur. Maybe the house wasn't quite so big. Maybe the cherry Cokes weren't that sweet and free-flowing. Maybe the drive-in movies, sandlot baseball, and rope swing at the swimming hole were all figments of Mitch's imagination. And maybe it wasn't ten summers in a row, but just a few summers in total.

But that coffee can was definitely real. Decades later, that memory inspired their own family tradition. Before vacations, Mitch and his wife, Sheila, would bring out the big glass apple cider bottle in which they had been faithfully depositing their own pocket change. Dumping it out, they'd divide the coins among their own four kids for personal spending money, always telling the story of Nana, Scottsburg, the coffee can, the cherry Cokes, and other memories that may have been romanticized over the years.

I have no idea whether you have the ability or inclination to invite a young crew of siblings or cousins to your place for a month or a long weekend. In this day and age, you probably can't leave them to fend for themselves for hours at a time, even if you live in a small midwestern town. But it's something to consider.

It's also important to consider some of the other less obvious lessons from Mitch's annual summer adventure. Such as, parents need an occasional break that grandparents can provide. Like no one else, you have the opportunity—and maybe the obligation—to connect with young people on a regular basis. Also, childhood adventures do not require investing thousands of dollars on cruises, ski lodges, and all-inclusive resort vacations.

In the end, more important than crystal-clear memories are the impressions we hold on to when the generations give of themselves. Love, laughter, tastes, sights, sounds. Brothers, sisters, cousins, friends. Warm summer nights. And a blue jean pocket filled with Nana's quarters, dimes, and nickels. •

You never forget
the way to
Grandma's house.

24

KEEP A GRAND-PARENTING BUCKET LIST

What follows is not an obligatory list of things you must do. Consider these ideas to be mere thought-starters. Some require months of planning and financial investment. Some—by putting down this book—you can do right now.

A number of these items will bring instant laughter; others may lead to thoughtful life-altering discussions. Some you can do in an afternoon; some are lifelong projects. A few require physical strength and stamina, others will tax your brainpower, and several do both. Some you can do with toddlers; others you will want to save until your grandchild is a teenager.

Most are fun, while some are quite serious. You may want to pull out a highlighter and select all those you simply don't want to miss. Don't forget to bookmark this page.

Presenting—in no particular order—a bucket list for grandparents like you.

- Plant a tree.

- Go fishing.

- Play checkers. Play chess.

- Play rock, paper, scissors.

- Roast marshmallows, tell ghost stories, and eat junk food late into the night.

- Play trampoline basketball.

- Pitch a tent in the backyard.

- Tour your local fire station.

- Go through a car wash. Open the window for one second.

- Do a fast-food progressive dinner. Salad at one place. Tacos at the next. Burgers at another. Finish at an ice-cream shop.

- If you know anyone who owns a restaurant, mechanic shop, or other small business, take your grandkids on a behind-the-scenes tour.

- Try go-karting.

- Go zip-lining.

- Drive bumper cars.

- Create an obstacle course in your backyard and hold a competition between siblings and cousins. Chart personal best times.

- Have a picnic in the living room. Throw a blanket down, open a picnic basket, and tell stories about "the way things used to be."

- Entertain toddlers with bubble wands, block towers, peek-a-boo, or follow-the-leader.

- Erect a basketball hoop in your driveway.

- Stage squirt gun battles.

- Catch and release butterflies or lightning bugs.

- Watch a hot-air balloon launch. Take a hot-air balloon ride.

- Go to classic car shows.

- Go to homecoming football games.

- Enjoy free music in the park. Splurge for overpriced pop star concerts.

- Look for four-leaf clovers.

- Chase a tornado.

- Teach them poker. Take their money.

- Run a marathon. Or half-marathon. Or 5K.

- Walk behind a waterfall.

- Ride the subway or elevated tracks.

- Solve a Rubik's Cube.

- Visit Stonehenge.

- Walk across Abbey Road with three grandkids.

- Take selfies. (Forbid duck faces!)

- Read bedtime stories.

- Tell them stories of when you were little.

- Start a file folder for each of your grandkids. Insert greeting cards, printed programs with their names, scribbles on printer paper, or anything that's two-dimensional.

- Frame one of their most creative works of art.

- Fly a kite. Build a kite.

- Build a model rocket.

- Write a poem. Write haiku.

- Go to the library and explain the Dewey Decimal System.

- Make shadow puppets.

- Put on a puppet show.

- Get a big jar and fill it with sand and ants for a homemade ant farm.

- Visit their great-grandma.

- Visit the older lady down the street.

- Visit a cemetery.

- Hold a tea party.

- Play twenty questions.

- Start a blog.

- Carve a pumpkin. Carve a potato.

- Lay out a Frisbee golf course in your neighborhood or nearby park.

- Fill a photo album.

- Make tie-dye T-shirts.

- Learn a magic trick.

- Memorize a favorite poem, quotation, or psalm.

Hooray for

- Play kick the can, spud, ghost in the graveyard, or capture the flag.

- Play hopscotch, ring around the rosy, or hide-and-seek.

- Do leaf rubbings. Do gravestone rubbings.

- Identify birds.

- Memorize the presidents and recite them as fast as you can.

- Learn the Greek alphabet.

- Learn the American Sign Language alphabet.

- Skip rocks.

- Riffle through your old baseball-card collection. Buy five new packs.

- Make paper airplanes or a cootie catcher.

- Cut snowflakes from white printer paper.

- Build a snowman. Make snow angels.

- Build a sandcastle.

- Run through the sprinkler. Run through a pile of leaves.

- Be daring. Stand up on a toboggan. Cannonball off the high dive.

- Go to your office and make photocopies of your faces.

- Spin a potter's wheel.

- Visit a shooting range.

- Create mild explosions.

- Catch frogs, snakes, and chipmunks.

- Count the rings in tree stumps.

- Stop at a construction site and identify the different types of Caterpillar earthmovers: backhoes that scoop, front loaders that lift, bulldozers that push.

- Take a horse-drawn carriage ride.

- Go to a rodeo, monster truck rally, symphony, or model train show.

- Do Disney.

- Take a road trip to the Grand Canyon, Everglades, Rock and Roll Hall of Fame, Alamo, or Cooperstown.

- Do an organized Road Scholar® Grandparents learning adventure.

- Visit your old high school or college campus.

- Do the must-see touristy sights in your own hometown.

- Give piggyback rides, noogies, whisker rubs, and butterfly kisses.

Hooray for

- Walk in the park and stop to chat on a bench.

- Sign up for a family trivia contest. Impress them with your wisdom.

- Coach their sports teams, lead their Scout troop, or volunteer to teach Sunday school.

- Rent a lakeside cabin or ski chalet.

- Save up for a family-friendly cruise.

- Follow your favorite baseball team to spring training.

- Book a lodge at a national park.

- See how many mini-marshmallows you can catch in your mouth.

- Take a Segway tour.

- Rent bikes, tandem bikes, canoes, or kayaks.

- Go horseback riding, rock climbing, white water rafting, or cross-country skiing.

Grandma and Grandpa, there are opportunities for teachable moments every time you see your grandchildren. But always make sure to leave room for a little fun. Your grandchild's snowman doesn't have to be the biggest. The go-kart you make together doesn't have to qualify for Daytona. You don't have to explore every room of that museum. Push your grandkids and yourself a little, but not too far out of your comfort zone. Find joy in the simple pleasures. ●

Give your grandkids so many memories that they never run out of stories about how awesome you were.

25
DISPELLING STEREOTYPES

Anytime you can tear down a wall of prejudice for your grand-kids, you're doing them a great service. One "ism" you can defend against without too much effort is ageism.

Research by R. N. Butler in *The Gerontologist* (1969) revealed that negative stereotypes against older people can begin as early as three years and may lead to discrimination, segregation, and disregard. And a study by R. J. and J. D. G. Goldman in the 1981 *Australian Journal of Psychology* found that school-age children often associated older people with a decline in physical and psychological capacities, such as deterioration of skin, bones, posture, hearing, and thinking power, as well as bad temper, impatience, and inability to cope with stress.

However, all is not bleak with how young people assess seniors. The 2018 study "Generations Learning Together" in the *Journal of Intergenerational Relationships* revealed that while preschoolers described older people as suffering from health challenges, they were still good playmates. Older adults also were perceived as having a higher amount of warmth, according to a 2012 *Journal of Personality and Social Psychology* article, "A Model of (Often Mixed) Stereotype Content," which includes traits such as being kind, friendly, and trustworthy.

So, grandparents, if you truly want to be worthy of a hearty hooray, you have a meaningful assignment. Even if you don't think of yourself as a playmate filled with warmth, dedicate some effort to taking advantage of that positive perception. Play with your grandkids. Build on that friendship and trust. Confirm your warmth and kindness. At the same time, combat the negative stereotypes so you and your peers are less likely to be subjected to discrimination and disregard. Watch your temper. Do a little less complaining about your aches and pains. Be intentional about standing tall and thinking through bits of advice before rendering your opinion. If you need a hearing aid or new prescription for your glasses, make that happen. In other words, don't be a grump—especially around your grandkids, who are already exposed to enough prejudice in this world.

AGE-BASED DISCRIMINATION

Two of the culprits that may be perpetuating ageist stereotypes are the media and your own children.

Of course, scriptwriters and newscasters are eager to depict Grandma as crabby or Grandpa as forgetful. Producers have already decided that nobody wants to watch a film or television program that portrays older characters as perfectly healthy with sound mind and body. For some reason, Hollywood thinks an old man shouting, "Get off my lawn!" is amusing. Ugh.

There's also a good chance your own adult children are having conversations—often with your grandchildren within earshot—that include either worries or exasperation about you. That's a naturally occurring turn of events because they're busy with their own responsibilities, deadlines, and occasional health issues. It's not a given, but your adult children might be seeing your frame of mind and current needs (differences of opinion, required visits, judgmental attitude, and health concerns) as unwanted hassles and obligations.

If all that seems unfair, I would have to agree. But you can't change the media and you can't even change your kids. The one thing you can do is choose not to give in to the stereotype and, maybe, showcase the exact opposite.

Does that sound like work? It might be. While you may not be responsible for ageism, you have a real chance to dispel those negative perceptions. Wouldn't it be rewarding for your grandchildren and their friends to look at your age group not as a burden, but as a blessing? What if they didn't see an entire generation that was past its prime and usefulness, but a resource-filled wave of valuable experience and continuing curiosity? What if every interaction you had with your kids and grandkids left them feeling lucky, blessed, and delighted that you are in their lives?

I know what you're thinking. *What? I need to put a smile on my face and exude a constant positive vibe, which might even mean hiding some of my own aches, pains, and frustrations? I need to keep any opposing opinions to myself? I need to make sure that every interaction begins and ends with smiles and gratitude? I need to give without expectation? You're telling me I need to be . . . delightful?*

Well, yes. That's exactly the recommendation of this chapter. Accept that proposal and I can (almost) promise you that visits will be easier and more frequent. Your family will enjoy you more. And you'll enjoy them. When the media paints grandparents as ill-tempered curmudgeons, your kids and grandkids will not even recognize that trope.

This short chapter is not suggesting you deny the effects of aging. In general, your children and grandchildren should be kept aware of significant ailments, losses, frustrations, and physical challenges as they come along. The secret might be to not let those setbacks define you. Maintaining a sense of humor and optimism is a better choice.

Think of it this way: Your adult kids don't want to think of you as old. Because when you're gone, they're next! If possible, for this next season of life, find the joy. Be optimistic. Even winsome. Make this current satisfying season last as long as possible.

The goal is that—a few years from now—when you do need a bit more help, you will have laid the groundwork for your kids and grandkids to rally around you, eager to give back to the wonderful, loving family matriarch and patriarch that have done so much for so long. •

You're only as old
as your grandkids
think you are.

26
SAY YES SO YOU CAN SAY NO

Say yes to your adult children as much as possible. "Yes, we would love to watch Judah and Gideon so you can go to a movie." "Yes, you can store your collection of Raggedy Ann dolls in your old bedroom." "Yes, we can delay our family holiday gathering a week so you can spend the actual holiday with your in-laws." "Yes, I can drive your family to the airport." "Yes, I can sew Jackson a Batman cape for Halloween." "Yes, I'll build a dollhouse for Emerson."

It's fun to say yes. And it's often not a big deal or a big sacrifice. For the most part, saying yes to a request from your kids or grandkids strengthens your connection and builds trust and confidence. You're glad to do it, especially if it's in your area of giftedness. Any *yes* you give is much appreciated.

There's another unspoken benefit of saying yes. Being a grandparent who typically says yes makes it a little easier, when necessary, to say no. Saying no is not nearly as fun. But it's equally as important, perhaps even more so.

One of my first memories of my own fatherhood was visiting my parents with our firstborn, Alec, when he was just a few weeks old. Rita and I had been trying to figure out whether she would be able to be the best mom in the world while also juggling some kind of income-producing career. Sitting in my parents' kitchen, I broached the topic of their availability as regular babysitters.

My dad, who clearly loved Alec more than anything in the world, took a moment to consider the magnitude of the request. Finally, he said, "We will be there for anything you need. Anytime, anyplace. But please, let's not intentionally create a situation in which our grandson is a burden to us."

In the moment, my dad's reply felt a bit harsh. But we soon realized it was brilliant. There was a lot of love and thought in that statement. There was also a promise and a challenge. Allow me to explain.

At the time, neither of my parents was yet retired. Dropping off an infant under their care several times per week would have been impossible. Their season of life just didn't allow for that kind of responsibility. That being said, I also knew—without a doubt—that if tragedy struck and my parents had to step up and raise little Alec, they would have made his welfare their top life priority.

In addition, my father's words were a challenge we needed to hear and led to a critical decision for Rita and me in our role as new parents. Simply stated, our children were our responsibility. For sure, we were in our early twenties. We had much to learn. We would struggle balancing budgets and schedules. But raising a family was not something you could do halfway or sidestep. You had to be all in.

Do your children—the parents of your grandchildren—know that? Do they know and accept their primary role as caretaker and provider? I hope they do. Unfortunately, that expectation is not something you can blurt out in the middle of a dinner conversation. Shrieking "I already raised my kids, now it's your turn" at young parents is not a good option. That conversation would not end well.

Instead of that painful verbal exchange, let's go back to the premise of this chapter. Whenever possible, say yes. Say it often. Step up heroically and be a generous, involved, and bighearted grandma and grandpa. Once you establish that magnanimous attitude, then you will feel free and empowered to say, "I'm so sorry. That's not something we can help with."

Let me quickly add that every season of life and all grandparents are different. When our grandbabies came along, Rita was in the exact right position to say yes to holding those babies for a few hours a few times per week. Our sons and daughters-in-law have been very grateful.

Let me also add, our grown children have made requests to which we've said no as well. Consider this chapter permission for you to do the same. ●

27

SEVEN CREATIVE PROJECTS

The highly energized two-dimensional world of handheld tablets and big-screen TVs may seem to inspire creative thinking, but experts say it might be just the opposite. A multiyear study on adolescent brain cognitive development by the National Institutes of Health uncovered volumes of data and warnings regarding children's increased exposure to digital screens.

Findings in the 2018 article "Is Screen Time Altering the Brains of Children?" in *Healthline* confirm that children who reported more than two hours a day of screen time got lower scores on thinking and language tests. Also, MRI scans found significant differences in the brains of children who reported using smartphones, tablets, and video games more than seven hours a day.

None of this should come as a surprise. Saturday morning cartoons of the mid-twentieth century seem like still-life paintings compared to today's fast-paced digital offerings for children. Plus, we grew up with one TV set that never left the family room instead of a handheld device that begs for our grandchildren's attention on every car trip, outing, appointment, queue, beach excursion, or visit to Grandma's.

Admittedly, the images on those phones and tablets are the *result* of creativity by graphic digital designers. The images and audio may even be inspiring! But let's also admit that the young people using those devices are not sharpening their imagination or developing any creative skills of their own.

That might be where grandparents can step up and step in. Busy and distracted parents may use screens as a babysitter or give up and give in to how older kids are using screens. But let's make sure the time we spend with our grandkids is not wasted by allowing them to have their heads slumped over into that digital dungeon.

You can't scream "Put down your darn phone!" Which means the challenge is to come up with fascinating and compelling alternatives that will have your grandkids *voluntarily* holstering their screens to engage with something hands-on and legitimately creative.

BUILDING A LEGACY

My seven-year-old grandson was in our upstairs playroom playing with the wooden Noah's Ark designed to fit our sizable collection of Beanie Babies. I realized it could be a nice moment to connect Jackson with his great-grandfather, who had passed just two years before he was born. "Papa made that," I told Jackson, "That's my dad."

Then, looking around the room, I suddenly became aware that we were surrounded by a wooden table, rocking elephant, Matchbox car ramp, step stool, dollhouse, art easel, and Noah's Ark all crafted with love by my father years ago for my own kids. Overcome with emotion, I pointed out each of those handmade wooden creations to Jackson. With sudden determination, Jackson stood up and said, "Let's go, Chief. I need to meet him!"

I gasped at the idea and the innocence of my grandson's request, and found myself overwhelmingly grateful for my father's legacy—one I had not previously fully recognized. I told my grandson, "Well, Jackson, Papa's in heaven, and one day you will meet him. But isn't it great that part of him is still right here? In all this stuff he made . . . and in me . . . and in you?"

Hooray for

None of these ideas will come as a complete surprise. Feel free to add to this list. All you really need to do is think back to the stuff that fascinated you back in the day.

1. Build stilts. If you're an old woodworker, you can imagine these already. Find or buy a couple of 6-foot (1.8 m) pieces of 1x2 pine for the poles. Attach triangles of wood for the footrests and watch your grade-school-age grandchild grow tall enough to look you in the eye.

2. Invest in an art easel. For less than fifty bucks you can supply your grandchild with high-quality paint, brushes, paper, and an easel. The result is hours (and years) of creative play. And maybe a new hobby for you as well.

3. Get creative with cookery. Let them page through one of your old cookbooks. Find a recipe, do the shopping, and whip up a dish that neither of you has ever made before.

4. Learn origami. It's trickier than it looks. And some kids really, really get into it. Start with regular white printer paper and some online tutorials. Be prepared to invest in colored paper designed specifically for the purpose of elegant and imaginative paper folding.

5. Start a family band. Gather harmonicas, kazoos, tambourines, maracas, recorders, and xylophones, one for each kid of any age, including grandparents.

6. Make something temporary. On the beach, create a sandcastle. In the family room, build a fort with pillows, couch cushions, and blankets. (Use an upside-down laundry basket as a lookout turret.) Repurpose that giant cardboard appliance box into a castle, spaceship, or clubhouse. Cut out windows, doors, peepholes, and ramparts. Decorate with paints or markers. In a week, toss it in the recyclables.

7. Build something that lasts. Make a treehouse, go-kart, dollhouse, game table, rocking horse, or skateboard ramp. Choose a project that may take more than a day to design and build. And really do it right.

Beyond these ideas, consider some of the skills you've developed (and maybe forgotten) over the years. Do you know how to juggle, whistle with your fingers, hang a spoon from your nose, draw caricatures, twist balloon animals, play the spoons, or do a few simple magic tricks? Pass it on!

For some of these suggestions, you may have to do a Google or YouTube search for instructions. But other than that, power down any screen as quickly as possible. •

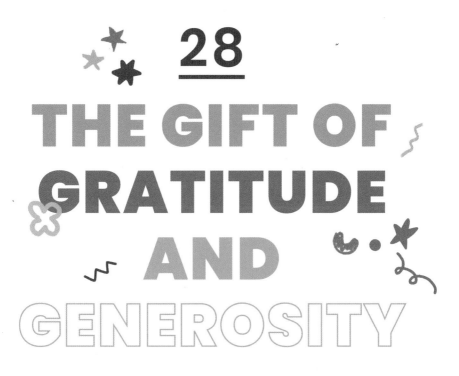

28
THE GIFT OF GRATITUDE AND GENEROSITY

On Thanksgiving several years ago, our neighbors Ron and Rebecca gave their children and grandchildren a great gift. They announced they no longer needed Christmas presents. Instead, they gave each of those three growing families an envelope with a small check and an assignment. (The amount of money doesn't really matter, it's the concept that is most meaningful.)

Ron and Rebecca requested that what they really wanted for Christmas was a story. A story of how God led each family to share this gift and the impact it had.

Of course, those grandparents had been praying and thinking about this adventure for many months and were prepared to lay out minimal ground rules. The money could be given outright in one lump sum to a worthy charity. Or it could be given out a few dollars at a time to scores of individuals who had a need. Each family could decide together what to do. The most important rule was that when they gathered for Christmas, the story of how the money was disbursed was to be shared with the entire family.

It wasn't a contest. It wasn't a test. It wasn't meant to be a hassle, puzzle, or burden for those families. As explained by Ron and Rebecca, they were hoping to do two simple things with this idea. They wanted to help instill the values of generosity and gratitude in their children and grandchildren. And, personally, they wanted to give back to God what he had so generously given them over the years.

The results have been powerful and eternal. Each year, as you can imagine, shared stories bring smiles, laughter, cheers, tears, and hearts filled with hope for the coming generations. Anonymous presents have been delivered. Families celebrated. Strangers surprised. Parents in tough situations were able to meet the needs of their kids. And so on.

They called the annual experience their "Family Journey of Generosity Gift." Just as Ron and Rebecca had hoped, they confirm that the best gift was how their entire family has a new awareness and appreciation of the true meaning of Christmas. As happens so often, when practicing generosity, the blessings return a hundredfold.

The journey has evolved over the years. Some years the children and grandchildren have added their own matching gifts. One year the entire clan was led to pool their resources on one larger project. Not surprisingly, the young families have become more aware of the needs around them throughout the year as they contemplate how they will share the generosity gift each coming Christmas.

When the holidays come around, feel free to steal some version of this idea for your family. It doesn't have to revolve around religion. The amount of money isn't critical, but it should be enough to generate a bit of excitement with your crew.

The side benefit is also obvious. As grandparents, you won't have to spend Christmas morning oohing and aahing over nonessential knickknacks, redundant appliances, articles of clothing you'll never wear, and other gifts you really don't need.

Another option would be, instead of disbursing a financial gift, mobilizing your entire family to give their time or talents to others. Also, the activity doesn't have to center on any one holiday. Right in your area are charities, churches, synagogues, food banks, shelters, schools, park districts, and agencies that could use some extra hands at any time of the year. Imagine witnessing every member of your extended family volunteering together for a few hours at a worthy charity. What a blast! What a lesson!

Many of the chapters in this book encourage grandparents to do things that connect with their grandchildren. This idea goes one step further. You're enlisting your kids and their kids to engage their own hearts, minds, and bodies in service to others. That inspires empathy, creativity, and selflessness—all good stuff the world needs a little more of. ●

29

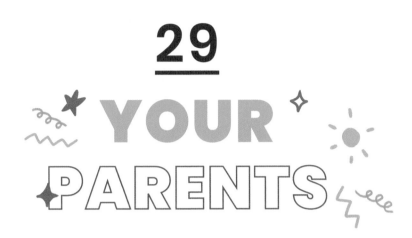

YOUR PARENTS

If you're a young grandparent, there's a good chance that another generational layer is part of your family. Which means you're not just a parent and grandparent, but you are also still an active son or daughter.

As you already know, watching out for the welfare of older parents can bring all kinds of stresses and expectations to your life—perhaps on a daily basis. As great-grandparents—now in their seventies, eighties, or nineties—your mother and father are passing on the generational baton. You need to be prepared to accept it.

Many decisions and obligations beginning to fall on your shoulders have far-reaching implications. The entire extended family may be expecting you to claim your role as the focal point for gatherings and to carry on family traditions. You may get a lot of conflicting input, but ultimately the decisions regarding where and when to hold family holidays and vacations are yours.

Moreover, you likely will be making difficult decisions about your parents. That includes their living arrangements, the disposition of their old house, and their long-term accommodations. Along

HOORAY FOR GREAT-GRANDPARENTS

There can be something just a bit magical about a six-year-old interacting with a great-grandparent. Not to reinforce stereotypes, but there's a moment in the arc of those two life spans when a youngster may be *learning* new things and an octogenarian may be *forgetting* a few things. All of which means they can be equal companions on the road of life. Those two family members—separated by three generations—may find common ground talking about the surprising deliciousness of a dish of sherbet, the intricacy of a spiderweb, or the croaks coming from a nearby frog pond. Parents, teenagers, and most members of the family don't have the time or patience for such silly distractions. But with a little preparation and patience, you can orchestrate those satisfying moments between your grandkids and your own parents.

with that comes health care, medications, and even the task of transporting your parents and in-laws to doctors' appointments. Plus, there are myriad financial decisions, such as establishing power of attorney and estate planning.

It's not just time-consuming, it's exhausting. And it's potentially fraught with conflict between siblings and other family members. Consider yourself warned.

If you find yourself in this position, also consider yourself blessed. You've been given the opportunity to give back to your parents, set some precedents, and model appreciation, devotion, and loyalty. Approaching this season of life with patience and humor will be a great gift to your entire family.

You may find yourself making regular visits to the house in which you grew up, a place to which your parents downsized, or some kind of retirement village. When possible, drag along one or two of your own grandchildren. Great-grandparents need to see evidence of their unfolding legacy. It provides a wonderful opportunity to brighten the week for all involved and it's really okay if sometimes both the little ones and the seniors get names and relationships confused.

For your part, see if you can keep the conversation upbeat. Ask open-ended questions of your mom or dad that help uncover a few unspoken memories. Too often, time with older seniors includes idle talk about the weather or rehashing their latest physical ailments. Great-grandkids don't want to hear that. Keep the conversation going until the family patriarch or matriarch tells a story that even you have never heard before. Don't delay. Those memories fade when you least expect it.

Finally—and I'm sure you've thought of this—the way that you look after your parents will have a significant impact on the way your own children will look after you. ●

Never forget, your children may someday choose your nursing home.

30

27 OPEN-ENDED QUESTIONS

Questions can get your grandkids talking. Especially recommended are open-ended questions with no right or wrong answer. They can get your grandkids imagining, sharing unexpected details of their lives, and practicing the skill of making choices.

With a few gentle prompts, they may begin to reveal some of their innermost thoughts. Ask these questions whenever you find yourself waiting in line, driving in a car, or enjoying a meal or snack. Or deliver them via text or on a phone or FaceTime call. If you're tucking in, go ahead and turn out the light and let the stillness prompt an engaging conversation that lasts for quite a while.

Consider these twenty-seven questions a starting point. Skip those that don't resonate with you. Feel free to creatively come up with your own questions too. If it goes well, seek out other sources, including books, questions cards, and the ever-present internet.

Oh yeah, don't just ask questions. Really listen to the answers. And don't be surprised if they start asking you questions of their own!

1. What's something unusual that happened today?

2. What has been your favorite vacation ever?

3. If your pet (or stuffed giraffe) could talk, what would it say?

4. What is something you're really thankful for?

5. If you had a camera, what would you have taken a picture of today?

6. What do you do well that you wish you could do even better?

7. Would you rather have a treehouse, an underground fort, or a secret room in the house? Why?

8. What's the funniest sound you can make?

9. Would you rather be the best player on a team that lost all their games or the worst player on a team that won all their games?

10. What's something you've never done but want to try?

11. What's the best thing about our family?

12. What do you know about my mom and dad? (Your great-grandparents!)

13. What are you looking forward to most about being a teenager?

14. Why do you think that car ahead of us is going so fast?

15. Why do some kids smoke or do drugs?

16. What would the world be like if everyone carried around a helium balloon on a string everywhere they went?

17. How do you show someone you care about them?

18. What would you imagine God to be like?

19. What's something you used to be scared of, but aren't anymore?

20. What is your family's favorite meal?

21. What makes our family special?

22. What are three things you look for in a friend?

23. What are three things you want to do this summer? Or this school year?

24. If you could have one superpower, what would it be?

25. What's your favorite spot in this house? Why?

26. What is something you can do tomorrow that you've never done before?

27. What is something that I should do more of? Or stop doing?

When young people begin to share their opinions and preferences, it's important not to make negative judgments. You want them to feel free to speak candidly. You want them to open up, not close down. That's especially important when you're talking about hopes and dreams. A grandparent saying, "Well, that will never happen!" or "You shouldn't think about things like that!" can shut down the imagination or vulnerability of a young person. That's the exact opposite of the reason you're asking these kinds of questions.

Of course, if this fun exercise does reveal some concerns about the safety and health of your grandchild, make note of what they say and how they say it. Moving forward, decide whether, when, and how you should bring others into this circle of confidence. The trust you've built with your grandkids is valuable, but their well-being is even more so. ●

When you know your grandchild, you better know yourself.

31

27 QUESTIONS THAT HAVE ANSWERS

As experienced in the previous chapter, asking open-ended questions with no right or wrong answer can get your grandchildren imagining and revealing unexpected insight into their lives.

Equally important are questions that have specific answers. Kids need to know that there are absolutes in this world. There is a difference between facts and opinions. Many questions they will face in life have right answers and wrong answers.

There's nothing like a good brainteaser to engage your grandkids.

1. What's the closest star?

2. Name two kinds of animals with eight legs.

3. Why are firetrucks red?

4. How many words can you make by rearranging all four letters in the word *stop*?

5. What are two things you can never eat for breakfast?

6. How can you tell the difference between pennies, nickels, dimes, and quarters with your eyes shut?

7. How many squares are on a checkerboard?

8. When you take two apples from three apples, what do you have?

9. Why are there little bumps on the "J" and "F" keys of most keyboards?

10. Why are manhole covers round?

11. Does ice sink or float in water?

12. What is the only flying mammal?

13. What's unusual about the sentence "Step on no pets"?

14. Where did the word *scuba* come from?

15. Who was the first person to set foot on the moon? What year?

16. Why do things fall when you drop them?

17. How old do you think I am?

18. Whose faces are carved on Mount Rushmore?

19. What shape is a stop sign?

20. What are the three phases of matter? Name each of those phases for H_2O.

21. What letter in the alphabet is not found in the names of any US states?

22. What is the world's tallest mountain?

23. How many cubic feet of earth are there in a hole 2 feet wide, 3 feet long, and 4 feet deep?

24. Why was six afraid of seven?

25. In baseball, what are the seven ways a batter can get to first base?

26. What word do you see when you print the word *swims* upside down?

27. What are my mom and dad's names? (Your great-grandparents!)

Asking questions is a classic tool in education, moral grounding, and self-discovery. Famously, Socrates taught by asking questions, thus establishing the Socratic method of testing logic and making reasoned arguments.

Jesus concluded many of his parables with a question. He ended the story of the Good Samaritan with the question, "Now which of these three would you say was a neighbor to the man who was attacked by bandits?" (Luke 10:36). After being asked whether or not it is lawful to pay taxes to Caesar, Jesus refused to be outwitted, saying, "Show me a Roman coin. Whose picture and title are stamped on it?" (Luke 20:24).

Irish novelist James Stephens said, "We get wise by asking questions, and even if these are not answered, we get wise, for a well-packed question carries its answer on its back as a snail carries its shell."

In other words, the very act of asking questions is valuable, even if all it does is unite a child in a worthy quest for answers with Grandma or Grandpa. •

When your grandchild asks a question, dawdle over your answer so as to savor the scrutiny.

ANSWERS

1. The sun, of course.

2. Spiders, octopi, scorpions, lobsters, ticks, and others.

3. In theory, red is more visible in traffic. You may recall studies several decades ago had fire departments opting for lime green trucks.

4. Six! Stop, spot, tops, pots, post, and opts.

5. Lunch and dinner.

6. By the size and weight. Plus, pennies and nickels don't have ridges.

7. A mind-blowing 204 squares. Although when your grandchild says, "64," give them a positive affirmation, but then point out how the entire board is a square. They'll likely say, "Okay then, 65." That's when you ask them to consider "the next right answer."

8. You have two apples.

9. Touch typists place their pointer fingers on those bumps to begin typing without looking at the keys.

10. There are several advantages worth discussing. But the biggest reason is that the "lip" around the rim of the hole is slightly smaller than the round cover, preventing it from accidentally falling through.

11. Ice floats. Although only about 10 percent of an ice cube or iceberg remains above the surface.

12. The bat. (Flying squirrels really only glide.)

13. It's a palindrome, which is a word or phrase reading the same backward and forward.

14. It's an acronym for "self-contained underwater breathing apparatus."

15. Neil Armstrong in 1969.

16. Gravity.

17. Perhaps 29?

18. George Washington, Thomas Jefferson, Teddy Roosevelt, and Abraham Lincoln.

19. An octagon.

20. Solid, liquid, vapor. Ice, water, steam.

21. Q.

22. Mount Everest in Nepal. First climbed in 1953 by Edmund Hillary and sherpa Tenzing Norgay.

23. There is no dirt in a hole. It's a hole!

24. Because seven ate (eight) nine.

25. Hit, walk, error, fielder's choice, hit by pitch, dropped third strike, and catcher's interference.

26. SWIMS.

27. Your parents' names are probably not Zoe, Apple, Dweezil, River, Dakota, Ziggy, Seven, Wednesday, or Elon. ●

32
PULL OUT & YEARBOOKS

Somehow your children survived their teenage years and eventually gave you grandchildren. Well, here's your chance to pay them back for everything they put you through back in the day.

In preparation for the next time your grandkids stop by, pull out their mom or dad's old high school yearbook. It's probably in the bottom of that dusty corner bookshelf or shoved in a memory box left behind in the basement, attic, or guest room closet. (If you can't find it, then track down an equally embarrassing family photo album from those years.)

As your grandchild flips through the pages, the stories and question about their parents' high school days will naturally flow. *What's with that hair? Where did that nickname come from?*

What clubs were they in? Who was their best friend? Who did they go to prom with? Did they ever break their curfew? Dad said he played baseball, but he's not in the team photo.

If the yearbook has signatures and comments scrawled by your child's classmates, even better! Reading those handwritten comments, the journey back in time will be even more eye-opening for your grandkids. *Who's L.K. and why won't they ever forget what happened after the homecoming game? Where is "the cabin" mentioned by so many classmates? How come Mom went to concerts in the city, but I can't? When and where did "Dragon" puke and why was he sick? Whatever happened to all those kids who wrote, "Friends4ever!"?*

Some of these questions you can answer. Most of them will be brought home to their parents. Sound like fun? Actually, you'll be doing your adult children a favor. The scribbled memories of their classmates reveal some achievements your son or daughter can brag about, but also how they didn't always make the best decisions during their formative years. Yearbook entries divulge their academic achievements and involvement in clubs, sports, and other extracurricular activities that may not match the expectations they've presented to their offspring.

As a result, your grandson or granddaughter may accuse their parents of being slackers, partiers, geeks, or nerds. If everyone keeps their cool and maintains a sense of humor, some insightful revelations and relationship-building conversations may occur.

It's comforting for kids to imagine their mom or dad going through a certain amount of high school angst and teenage rebellion. That yearbook and some honest follow-up discussion might lead your grandchildren to an important revelation: *Maybe my parents do understand.*

While you're at it, don't forget to pull out your own yearbooks and photo albums. But be warned. You, also, may have some explaining to do. •

Never forget that grandparents and grandkids were once the same age.

33

BUY INTO THE BUSYNESS

Are your grandkids an unbelievable blur of busyness? That's not unusual. The culture feeds into a fast-paced lifestyle.

Almost all growing families seem to have jam-packed schedules and regularly race across town from one activity to the other. That includes every sport imaginable requiring team practices and individual lessons. Plus solo athletic activities and physical conditioning at a surprisingly early age. Beyond sports, kids are getting involved earlier and earlier in artistic, dramatic, and musical pursuits. Ancillary educational opportunities outside of school include foreign languages, private tutoring, library programs, and storefront learning labs. Your grandchildren may be signed up for valuable personal support classes for students who need a little help in some areas, as well as enrichment programs designed for top students to stay on top.

It's not unusual for kids—starting at four years old—to have close to a dozen can't-miss events on their schedule each week, with lessons in everything from archery to zither happening after school, early evening, after dinner, and all day Saturday and Sunday. Moms and dads have learned to strategically stay in close communication and jockey their own schedules around their children's activities. They wait in SUVs outside brick buildings parked in line with other parents ready to whisk kids to their next event. For dinner, they pick up fast food for fast lives. To say the least, life is nonstop.

I know what you're thinking. But really, fully engaged lives are probably okay. Maybe even a good thing. Children today are trying lots of activities never previously available and learning to adapt to change. In the process, they also learn to keep a schedule, to meet deadlines, and the importance of staying organized.

Busy kids aren't mindlessly vegging out in front of a television. Also, they never get bored or permanently discouraged. If one activity is frustrating or ends with tears, they don't have to wait long until another activity comes along and gives them another chance for success.

If this describes your grandkids, you may be wondering how you fit in and what role you should expect to play. First, promise yourself that you're going to express only excitement when they tell you about their daily and weekly adventures. It would be really easy—and not surprising—if Grandma or Grandpa felt the urge to express a negative opinion of their frenetic lifestyle. Please don't. As in most of the choices made by your own children when it comes to parenting, it just isn't a good idea to judge harshly or cast aspersions. If it's dangerous or life-threatening, that's one thing. Your input could be a difference maker. But for the most part, you'll want to go easy on making demands or recommendations simply because you have a

NURTURING YOUNG ARTISTS

Even if you're not an art connoisseur, grandparents can greatly encourage the creative side of their grandkids. Equally as important as their athletic schedules, make sure you get any and all artistic efforts on your calendar. In many cases, there's only one performance at the end of a season or semester. Bring a modest bouquet of flowers to congratulate the young dancer, violinist, vocalist, or actor. If they're part of a graphic arts exhibit— painting, drawing, sculpting, digital design, filmmaking—get in the habit of taking several minutes to silently observe or scrutinize their work. Nod your head, smile, express appreciation, and then ask open-ended questions like "Tell me about this" or "I'm wondering, do you have a vision for the finished artwork before the work begins or does the piece evolve during the creative process?" Treating them like a working artist—not a wannabe—is something you can do that most parents won't. You can't blame them. Moms and dads are way too distracted trying to imagine how art translates to a gainful career choice.

Hooray for

different perspective on their perfectly harmless activities, menu choices, sleeping schedules, and so on.

Second, when possible, show up and cheer! Insist you receive schedules of all games and performances. That being said, in a twenty-five-game season, please *don't* attend every soccer, baseball, or basketball game. You really should have other things to do and it's beneficial if little Joshua or Sadie occasionally looks to the bleachers and wonders where you are. But *do* make it to all the playoff and rivalry games that have special significance.

Finally, your biggest contribution to the life of a busy family could be filling in the gaps and being an extra driver or cheerleader. Especially when there are several kids in the family, parents literally cannot attend some events. If you can make yourself readily available to do a carpool pickup, shoot video, or make your grandchild feel supported, you'll be doing a welcome service.

Being part of the busyness is actually one of the joys of grandparenthood. What could be more important? Your involvement makes a difference. Being available and showing up will be greatly appreciated by your grandkids. And even more appreciated by their parents. ●

34

A GRANDKID- FRIENDLY HOME

Clearly, my grandparents didn't care about having a grandkid-friendly house. The carpet was white. The coffee table was glass. There were no games or children's books. Breakable knickknacks dangerously decorated every corner of the living area. They lived on a busy street and the one patch of grass wasn't big enough for a game of ring around the rosy.

What's more, I don't ever remember playing with Nana or Grandpa at that house. When we made the two-hour trip, for some reason we were usually all dressed in "good clothes." I could always count on a tasty meal around a formal dining room table, but most of the visit was several long hours of adults talking. My brother, two sisters, and I didn't mind going to Nana and Grandpa's, but we were also never sad to leave.

Two generations later, I cannot imagine that kind of relationship between grandparents and grandchildren. I don't mean to throw Fritz and Lillian under the bus, and maybe you experienced the same standoffish rapport with your grandparents. It was a different era, and in some families and cultural environments the prevailing wisdom was kids should be seen and not heard.

My own parents were significantly more engaged with all eleven of their grandkids—who always visited in playclothes and sneakers, expecting to have fun. Today, it seems routine for us to engage our two granddaughters and six grandsons in all kinds of hands-on activities. With newborns, that means rocking and swaying. In the years to follow, sitting cross-legged on the carpet playing with Lego, Matchbox, Playmobil, blocks, trains, and stuffed animals. Wrestling and tickling in the grass. Making s'mores in the backyard firepit. Cuddling up and reading storybooks or watching videos. We even had a sandbox one summer, which turned out to be not so popular with our daughters-in-law, who didn't appreciate sand ending up in shoes, socks, pants, and family vehicles.

As you consider your own home, I am 100 percent sure that you want it to be welcoming, inviting, joy-filled, and kid-friendly. With that in mind, there should be two parts to your plan.

FIRST, set aside a portion of your home for those young ones you love so much: a closet, trunk, corner of the family room, finished basement, kid-friendly backyard, or entire spare bedroom. You don't have to decorate the entire house in beanbag chairs and primary colors, but you do want the kids to be comfortable and safe, and have access to a few age-appropriate activities. Even if they only show up a few times a year, it's worth the effort, space, and investment.

SECOND, when they do come over, you certainly want to catch up with your grown children regarding whatever's going on in their lives. But you also want to carve out time specifically to enter the world of your grandchildren, whether one kid at a time or all of them at once.

Whatever activity they're doing, join in. But also—when they're at your home—introduce them to games you played when you were their age. Relive your own youth with hide-and-seek, running bases, checkers, marbles, go fish, spud, kick the can, capture the flag, hopscotch, four square, or duck, duck, goose. You can imagine how having some sidewalk chalk, a deck of cards, and other toys and supplies might be advantageous.

Over the years, my wife has convinced me to build a firepit, create a fairy garden, and put up a tree swing, ninja line, and zip line outside. Inside, we've got a dollhouse, bunk beds, Ping-Pong table, art easel, small performance stage, and several jam-packed bookshelves and games cabinets.

Follow through with your own plan to make your home fun, safe, and kid-friendly. When any of my children announce, "We're going to Grandma and Chief's house this weekend," I have it on good authority that our grandkids respond with cheers of delight. ●

35

A TEACHABLE MOMENT MISSED

While there wasn't much to do at Nana and Grandpa's house, the one corner of the old house we were allowed to explore was Grandpa Fritz's workbench. After an unfortunate turn of events, even that would become off-limits.

On one visit, my brother Mark and I had been in the dank basement playing "secret agent" and pretending one of Grandpa's unusual tools was a machine gun. As part of our game, we happened to hide that basin wrench under a chair cushion, and there it remained for weeks afterward. Eventually, Grandpa needed that specialized tool and was upset with himself for misplacing it.

Later, the wrench was found, and immediately Mark and I became prime suspects. After an accusatory and unpleasant long-distance phone call, we confessed to the crime and were promptly forbidden from touching any of Grandpa's tools again.

It wasn't until years later that I would learn what a basin wrench was used for. Looking back, I completely understand the old man's frustration, but it makes me sad that such a minor incident put up a wall that lasted, well, probably the entire final decade of our relationship. He never really seemed to let go of it—only adding to my feeling of guilt. At the time, Mark and I were goofy kids who made a mistake. A few years later we were teenagers with other priorities. Grandpa would pass away after I went off to college.

How might that relationship have turned around? How do I wish Fritz would have responded? It's easy to say now, but I can think of three ways that negative experience could have been turned into a positive. You may want to take notes.

FIRST, grandparents need to acknowledge that grandkids are kids. Mark and I were clearly at fault, but there was no animosity or evil intent behind our youthful lapse in judgment.

SECOND, taking that idea a step further, maybe—and stay with me here—grandparents should have the attitude that our grandkids can do no wrong. That may be a bit of an overstatement, but this idea suggests another way that grandparenting is so different than parenting. From a kid's perspective, Mommy and Daddy have all kinds of boundaries and establish consequences for poor decisions. But Grandpa and Grandma would never, ever lose their cool or dole out punishments. Even after the grape juice spills on the white carpet, the car keys are dropped down the sewer grate, or the boys playing in the basement hide Grandpa's basin wrench.

THIRD, when faced with a blunder by your grandchildren, see if somehow you can make it a teachable moment. This is another example of opportunities parents don't always have time or patience for. The lost-and-found basin wrench was a clear chance to pass on a life skill or lesson. After all, the tool had already grabbed the attention of two curious boys. In retrospect, there's no way Grandpa Fritz was going to climb under a sink and demonstrate how it works to Mark and me. But, in that same scenario, I can imagine my own father taking the time to describe to his grandchildren how a basin wrench can loosen or tighten fittings in hard-to-reach places. I'm not as handy as either of those men, but I am definitely a fan of teachable moments.

Of course, this chapter is not about basin wrenches. It's about leaving a legacy of positivity and how a single incident can damage a relationship. These words may also be a way for me to bring closure to my long-standing regret for shutting out and holding a grudge against my own grandfather. ●

36
RESPONDING TO OUR CHANGING CULTURE

Oh, the cultural upheaval you've seen in your lifetime. And there's surely more to come.

The challenge, of course, is that the members of society who have been around longest have witnessed the most radical change. And sometimes those genuinely wonderful individuals don't know how to handle it. The result is older generations are faced with confusion, possible anger, guilt, fear, self-doubt, and unexpected expectations. Initially, we may attempt to hold any disruption of status quo at arm's length. But often cultural shifts hit close to home and take people by surprise. Especially grandparents.

You didn't pick up this book expecting a debate on the pros and cons of the great cultural revolution of our time. So we're going to keep this chapter short. I offer two action items for maintaining strong family ties.

Let's be clear. You don't have to join demonstrations or marches. You don't have to put up yard signs, disavow your political party, or become a vegan. You don't have to change where you go on vacations, worship on weekends, or buy groceries. But you do have to commit to love.

As an elder statesperson of your family, you need to establish love as the first priority—for yourself and your entire clan. When a bit of unexpected news comes your way regarding a member or members of your family, extended family, or community, it's possible your *first* instinct is divisive, even destructive. That may be hard to admit. If potentially that's the case, then commit here and now to making sure your *second* impulse will be to love. Loving people you already love. Loving people you didn't think you could love. Loving your neighbor. Especially loving your grandkids.

What could be more important? What could be more effective when it comes to keeping open the doors of communication and the doors of your home? What's more, your demonstration of love may serve as a valuable model to many others.

The second part of the plan applies when the words coming out of your mouth sound disrespectful, antiquated, or even mean-spirited. Even though your goal is to love without limits, sometimes your personal history guides you down the wrong verbal or emotional path. Take a moment, and I'm sure you can recall your own parents or grandparents saying something totally inappropriate, perhaps using an offensive term or making a definitive statement that had long been proven to be untrue. Well, you've done—or will do—the same thing.

When that happens, younger members of your family may take you to task. They may groan, roll their eyes, or even verbally respond with their own counterattack. You meant no harm, but your words may have been hurtful.

The following suggestion on how you might choose to respond comes from an unlikely source. On a recent cross-country drive, I had tuned in to one of the comedy channels on Sirius radio and heard stand-up comic Orny Adams deliver a throwaway line that struck me as brilliant. It's a phrase I have found quite valuable and applies almost every time I find myself, well, saying something stupid.

Adams was doing a comedy bit on generational conflict and described how he responded to the sanctimonious judgment of twenty-somethings when he inadvertently made a comment offensive to their generation. He replied, "You're judging me on criteria I did not grow up with."

Does that rebuttal make sense to you? It does to me, and I encourage you to use some version of that phrase next time you are accused of being a boor or curmudgeon. While it sounds like an excuse, let's call Orny Adams's defense a reasonable explanation for our misconduct. Anyone paying attention should admit the rules seem to change every time we turn around, so maybe it's unfair to blame us if we don't have them all memorized.

Still, even though we are old dogs, we can learn new tricks. These new cultural standards are mostly reasonable, which means grandparents need to stop making excuses and keep trying to do better. In the meantime, let's all agree to double down on the first part of the plan: Love first. ●

Grandparents should always lead with love.

37
THE DOUBLE GIFT

Back when Rita and I were broke and raising two young sons, my parents stopped by more than once with a bag or two of groceries. They blamed the "buy one, get one free" offer at the supermarket that somehow led them to purchase more than they needed.

They insisted we would be doing them a favor by taking this food off their hands. After all, they didn't have room in their refrigerator and they didn't want it to go to waste.

My mom and dad knew I had a job that was not a good fit, but they never told me I was "wasting my life" or "clearly miserable." Even though that assessment would have been accurate. My work was, indeed, unrewarding and unfulfilling. What they did do was check in once in a while, make sure their grandsons were well fed, and treat their son like an adult.

They had faith Rita and I would figure out the best course of action for our little family. Honestly, I never felt judged or ashamed. My parents' quiet support was empowering. As part of a loving family, I had an assurance that my wife and sons would never lack for basic human needs. If the need arose, I knew I could ask my parents for financial help or career advice. But I also knew it was my job to figure out how to do something meaningful with my life that also paid the bills.

See how that worked? It's a double gift. It's grandparents helping, but the younger family preserving their pride. For me, that was hugely important. I will always be grateful, although I don't think I expressed it enough.

You may remember that feeling when your own children were born. Personal pride magnifies. Most new moms and dads want to be the sole providers for their new son or daughter. Sometimes that may not be the case and grandparents need to step in and do what's necessary for the health and well-being of the family. But in general, grandparents should give that growing family an opportunity to rise up to meet the challenge of self-sufficiency.

Make sense? I hope so.

Well, then, let's consider a few of the ways grandparents can become a silent partner in their adult children's honorable quest for independence.

FREE BABYSITTING If you live close, this is a no-brainer. It's a win-win. New parents need to get out occasionally and babysitters keep raising their rates. Even if you live far away, you can schedule visits in a way that allows you to watch your grandkids while Mom and Dad go out for a special event.

CAREER CONNECTIONS There's a high probability you are not in the loop when it comes to your son or daughter's career goals and skill set. That's okay. Still, in your wide circle of friends, former classmates, and business contacts, you might know someone who knows someone who could open a door or offer some guidance for their career path. Of course, all you're doing is passing on a contact. After that, get out of the way and let them follow through or not.

LOANING MONEY This is extraordinarily tricky. Simply put, don't lend money for general living expenses. Doing so opens the door for long-term dependency. On the other hand, do be receptive to the idea of investing specific amounts of money for a well-thought-out plan or onetime emergency. Bankrolling a legitimate business venture or helping with a down payment on a first home might be a risk worth taking. An emergency is, by definition, a predicament that only happens once. Steer clear of funding serial emergencies.

GIVE ADVICE ONLY WHEN ASKED Without a doubt, you have all kinds of wisdom to share on parenting, finances, home buying, car buying, marriage, lawn mowing, wallpapering, flossing, grilling, the best brand of peanut butter, and how to hang a new roll of toilet paper. But do your best to avoid offering unsolicited advice to adult children. It's unwelcome and customarily ignored anyway.

Moving forward, Grandma and Grandpa, that's your plan. One, be available. Two, honor their independence. It's a double gift. It's also a bit of a tightrope. In the end, you're really telling your adult children, "Hey, we're just the grandparents. You are more than ready to lead and provide for your own family." •

Few things are as satisfying as watching your children turn into parents right before your eyes.

38

BUY A MINIVAN

When my friend Mike turned sixty, he went out and bought a red Corvette to make him feel young again. It didn't work.

When my dad turned sixty, he went out and bought a minivan with lots of seat belts so he could take a pile of grandkids anytime, anyplace. It worked. All of which made him feel young again.

To be clear, he didn't purchase that vehicle to take the kids to the zoo or amusement park. That was never his style. My dad didn't like crowds or lines or spending money unnecessarily. He simply wanted to make sure that—when he felt like it—he could swoop into a couple of driveways and pick up two, three, four, five, six, or seven of his grandkids to go on routine trips to the supermarket or hardware store. With that minivan, one of his annual rituals was the practical but motivational mission of taking a gaggle of grandkids shopping for school supplies.

Still, it wasn't all errand running. Papa's vanload of grandkids would typically stop to get ice cream or feed the ducks. Maybe visit a pet store or local park. My dad had found a ministry of sorts—exposing

GRAMA ADVENTURE DAYS

I confess I have not yet been inspired to follow my father's example and initiate an ongoing series of outings known as "bumming with Chief." But I am happy to report that my partner in grandparenting has established a tradition that parallels Papa's legacy. The term "Grama Adventure Day" is tossed around with great joy and appreciation by our sons, daughters-in-law, and grandkids. Truth be told, it began as just a simple afternoon when Rita would babysit a single grandchild at a time. But somehow she makes it special. It could mean leaving the house to visit a craft store, supermarket, or local kid-friendly attraction. But often, it's simply Rita pulling out a secret stash of art supplies, twenty-year-old toys, or cookie-baking ingredients. Sometimes she even lets me join in her Grama magic. Once you label your outings— such as "adventure days" or "bumming"—it becomes more than babysitting. Plus, you'll start to hear those wonderful little voices asking, "Grama, what should we do on our next adventure day?"

his grandchildren to the adventures found in everyday life. He called it "bumming with Papa," and it might be his greatest legacy.

On the topic of minivans and seasons of life, Rita and I went through four minivans over the course of twenty-five years. When they first came out in the mid-1980s, we were one of the early adopters. Two decades later, we still were driving a minivan when most families were choosing SUVs. When the kids started getting older, we gave our last beat-up minivan to Max to drive during his last two years of high school and—surprise, surprise—Rita ended up with a new navy blue Chrysler Sebring convertible. That slightly frivolous vehicle was our second car for many years, marking our transition from "lot of kids at home" to "empty nesting."

What happened when grandkids came along? Well, you really can't put a car seat in a convertible. So, you guessed it. We traded in the old Sebring for another minivan. And we got new license plates: GRAMA 79. (Partially in honor of the year we were married.)

The kids and grandkids lovingly call that gray Dodge Grand Caravan the "Gramavan," which we joyfully fill up with six or eight family members for occasional field trips. (What nickname will your grandkids give to your minivan?) An added bonus is that the back seats come out pretty easily, which means Rita gets a call or text every few months asking, "Mom, can we borrow the

Gramavan?" It has become quite handy for moving small items of furniture or making a trip to the lumberyard.

Rita and I are more than happy we have a vehicle to meet that need. It's one more way we can come alongside our grown children and join them in this adventure called "family." ●

39
A GRAND-PARENTING EXERCISE

I do this once in a while. It's great fun. And eye-opening. To get the full effect—and find yourself laughing out loud—it probably helps if you have more than a few grandchildren. But it's also a valid exercise if you have one or two.

Here's the drill. Choose a grandkid and simply think about them until you smile. Their eyes, their hugs, their laugh, their serious face, the way they jump and wiggle, even the way they pout or whine. Imagine their future. Imagine the next time you get to see them.

That's it. Go ahead and try it.

If you've chosen a four-year-old grandson or granddaughter, it's easy. Your smile will come quickly. At that age, they are surprising, energy-filled goofballs that say very silly and sometimes very profound things.

Newborns also promote instant smiling. That's because they are all potential. The future has no limits. As they absorb the sights and sounds of the world, you can tell they are learning something every single moment. Babies and toddlers typically learn more in one day than you have in the last six months. Right?

Have a middle schooler in that upcoming generation? They are also going through moments of self-discovery. Plus, moments of rejection, frustration, and confusion. That's what middle schoolers are and what middle schoolers do. With that understanding, you should be able to smile knowing there's light at the end of the tunnel.

Thinking about the older teens or young adults in your family may leave you scratching your head. They are facing decisions you never even considered. Technology and culture have come so far. Still, you should be able to consider their heart, mind, and soul and find reason to smile.

Or maybe this exercise is hard. Smiling as you think about your grandchild may seem impossible. Some grandparents may even be angry reading this chapter. Why might that be?

Do you have grandchildren you don't know or can't know? Then this exercise is even more valuable than you realized. Perhaps this is a call to action to be more involved in that young life. If it requires some relationship mending or bridge building, then begin planning for how to make that happen. Search your heart. Set some new priorities. As the patriarch or matriarch of your family, you've been given the authority and responsibility to set the tone. It might not be easy. On the other hand, maybe it's not as difficult as you think. Consider doing what needs to be done so you—and many others—can smile again.

Maybe you stopped short in this "find-a-reason-to-smile exercise" because every time you think about one particular grandchild you get sad. In recent years that young person has been making some bad decisions and the idea of smiling about them doesn't seem remotely possible. That can be such a burden. Your heart is breaking and you feel helpless. Well, you are not helpless. Perhaps you are the help they need! You're still here. They're still here. Instead of involving the entire family, initiate a one-on-one connection with your grandson or granddaughter. What if you reached out and entered their life in a whole new way? You and them on a park bench. You and them taking a road trip. You and them finding the right doctor, social worker, or spiritual leader. You and them kicking back someplace with sun on your faces. Many young people just need someone who loves them to be the wind beneath their wings.

Here's another possibility. Maybe you can smile about all your grand-kids except one. That boy or girl has a physical, mental, or emotional challenge that you think holds them back. It makes you sad. Your dreams for them have fallen short. You pray for them and do internet research looking for answers. Their future, you think, is hopeless.

In that case—in every case—look closer. Think outside your box. Every child is different. And precious. Little Amelia or Elijah may not grow up to be a tech wizard, corporate CEO, or power-house attorney. But they may experience profound joy in ways that may be hard for you to understand. Do whatever it takes to share that joy.

Finally, maybe you cannot smile because one of your grandkids has left this world, and you don't want to think about him or her. As a grandparent, that's another gift you can bring to your family. Be the one who is not afraid—at the right time—to remember that precious life and express love and appreciation for what they meant to so many people.

This grandparenting exercise—pursuing a smile for each grandchild—is a private endeavor. But the result is more hope, appreciation, and joy in your life, which should be obvious to the entire family. Discovering or rediscovering each smile is a chance to clear away some of the darkness and fog, so you can envision a bright future for those young people you love so much. ●

*Love—especially
a grandparent's
love—can overcome
a multitude of
challenges.*

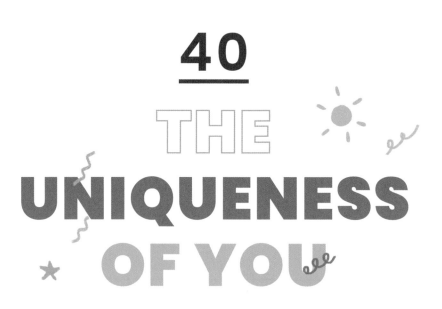

40

THE UNIQUENESS OF YOU

As we draw near the close of this book, let me talk for a moment to one grandparent at a time.

When it comes to each of your grandchildren, be yourself. Correction—be your *best* self. Take any one of your best traits and—when you're with your grandchild—let it shape your persona.

Examples? Be a hugger, smiler, friend, or confidant. Be a book reader, noogie giver, carpenter, or cookie maker. Be a gift giver or wise advice giver. Be a storyteller or joke teller.

Hooray for

Think of it this way: When they're in fifth grade, how do you want your grandson or granddaughter to describe you to their friends? "Oh, that's my granddad. He always has gum in his pocket." "Oh, that's my Nana. We hike together all the time."

Don't feel like you have to reinvent yourself. Instead, take an honest personal inventory. *Which of my gifts, traits, and abilities do I want to pass on to future generations?* Haven't thought about that in a while? Now's your chance.

Back in the day, you may have taken some kind of assessment test at school or early in your career. An afternoon of filling in tiny circles with a No. 2 pencil may have left you with a label that was extraordinarily accurate and led to open doors and new experiences. Or those test results may have crammed you into a box that never felt comfortable and from which you never escaped. In either case, consider it old news and no longer relevant.

Instead, take out a yellow pad or open a new Word doc. List the things that rock your world today. List the things you can do better than anyone else. List your core values. List the kind of things you want your grandson or granddaughter to remember about you, especially the ones you want them to emulate.

Got it? Is it a solid list? Are you nodding your head at some newly uncovered realizations? Excellent.

Now then, for the sake of your grandkids, consider retooling your life to bring those traits and talents to the surface. Present to the world and your family the best version of yourself. In the vernacular of today's youth, "You be you."

The decades past have passed. If you listen, you can hear the future calling your new name. (That voice, by the way, may sound a lot like your grandchild or grandchildren.) When you answer, step forward with that best version of yourself. That reinvigorated rendition may be one the world has never really seen before.

Who knew? •

Did you have any swings and misses as a mom or dad? Grandparenting just might be your chance for a do-over.

EPILOGUE:

COUNTING THE DAYS, MAKING THE DAYS COUNT

THIS WILL HAPPEN. You'll stop yourself in the midst of a busy day and think, *I wonder what the grandkids are up to. It's been a while.*

Then you start counting the days and realize it really has been a couple of weeks or months since you last spoke, hugged, or video chatted. It doesn't matter whether they live across town or two states away, you will find yourself feeling disconnected from those young people who mean so much to you. Worse, you begin to feel a bit guilty.

First, give yourself a break. There's a lot going on. Life happens.

Second, please don't make your son, daughter, son-in-law, or daughter-in-law feel guilty for not connecting more often. Their plates are undeniably full.

Third, make yourself a promise. Commit to reaching out on a regular basis with small moments of love and thoughtfulness. There are all kinds of subtle, amiable, and constructive ways to intentionally connect, ways that acknowledge their busy schedules without being disruptive or demanding. Your goal is to be a blessing.

Case in point: Your children and grandchildren may not have a free Saturday for months in a row, but a Thursday-evening pizza party may be quite welcome. Finding time for an hour-long Face-Time or Zoom call may be impossible, but exchanging emoji-filled texts (sometimes with pics attached) can bring smiles while catching everyone up on today's family news. With their sports and performance schedules on your phone, you have a complete list of prearranged opportunities to connect.

Grandparents who drive can volunteer to shuttle a grandchild to a crosstown event, which not only gives you time with them, but also becomes a gift of one less obligation for Mom and Dad. While you're in the car, find out what other errand you can help scratch off Mom and Dad's to-do list.

Also, remember that every visit doesn't have to include the entire family. Engaging with one grandchild at a time leads to special one-on-one moments and memories. It's quite possible your seven-year-old granddaughter would love to be liberated from her older brother's weekend soccer tournament.

Finally, not every outing or experience has to be fully orchestrated with jam-packed schedules, prepurchased tickets, landmark dis-coveries, or a huge financial investment. Often less is more.

One of the greatest gifts you can give your grandchildren is an afternoon away from the mayhem of twenty-first-century life. For sure, you know how to party with the best of them. But consider also taking a cue from grandparents of generations past. Read a book. Bake cookies. Build a birdhouse. Make s'mores. Count the stars. Lie in the grass and look for shapes in the clouds.

When life starts going a little too fast, your grandchild is counting on you to slow it down.

ABOUT THE AUTHOR

JAY PAYLEITNER spent a decade at three Chicago ad agencies writing and producing commercials for airlines, eggs, and Kroger supermarkets. He also led the creative team that named SunChips. Turning freelance, Jay spent two decades creating thousands of radio spots, specials, and PSAs for the Salvation Army, Prison Fellowship, American Red Cross, National Center for Fathering, and others. He served as executive director of the Illinois Fatherhood Initiative and speaks nationally on parenting, marriage, and finding your life purpose. Most notably, Jay has written more than twenty-five books, including *The Newlywed Year*, *52 Things Kids Need from a Dad*, *52 Ways to Connect as a Couple*, *Lifeology*, and *What If God Wrote Your Bucket List*? His books have been translated into ten languages and sold more than a half million copies. Jay and his high school sweetheart, Rita, live in the Chicago area, where they raised five awesome kids, loved on ten foster babies, and are cherishing grandparenthood. Find more about Jay at https://jaypayleitner.com.